MW01672415

"This is a great story of love, loss, suspense, the chilling unknown, and what regular people do when confronted with it."

-Stephen Millunzi

"PICTURES, DREAMS AND VISITS proved to be an interesting read. I'm not sure how much I believe, but you really presented a compelling argument."

-Margi Frank, Freelance Editor

"BEAUTIFUL...What a treasure this is!"

-Patricia Fatchett

"The pictures are truly remarkable and combined with your dreams and other experiences, tells a very special story."

-Father Bernard Reiser, Pastor,
The Church of the Epiphany

Pictures, Dreams and Visits

A True Story

Linda Graham
and
Betty Graham-Freiling

Gramus Publishing

Gramus Publishing.
P.O. Box 48187
Coon Rapids, Minnesota 55448-0187

ISBN: 0-9659122-0-5

PRINTED IN THE UNITED STATES OF AMERICA

Acknowledgments

We would like to thank our friends who so patiently listened, proof-read, supported and encouraged us to finish this effort: Betsy Zema-Sellers and Kathy Vesely.

Thanks to Kevin and Tom Donovan, author and illustrator of the "Billy Bear" book series and our cover designer and consultant, who helped make this book a reality.

A very special thanks to our families, whose patience was truly a God sent gift...Betty's husband Craig, her children Jim and Laura, and Craig's mother Bernice Freiling. Linda's children, Jennifer, Andy and Tom; Ron Busch, our Aunt Alma Hooverman and Pat's children, Rachel and Jared for their special contributions.

We are truly grateful to our step-mother, Audrey Graham-Scherf (fondly called Grandma John by her grandchildren) not only for her support and encouragement delivered by phone from 2,000 miles away, but for always being there for us because our mother couldn't.

And, we can't forget our cousin, Pat Botz.

This book is dedicated in loving memory to our parents

John and Irene Graham

and to our brother

Patrick John

TABLE OF CONTENTS

A NOTE FROM THE AUTHORS

I couldn't tell where the menacing sound was coming from. Was I in a forest? Even though I couldn't penetrate the darkness to make out any trees, I could feel spongy softness under my feet. It must be grass. I carefully tried to work my way out. And why? I had not asked to be here. To be where? I had no idea where or how I had gotten here, but I knew I had to get out before the sound came to get me. The sound came closer, but from what direction? I stopped abruptly and listened, ready to bolt in whatever direction would take me to safety, but I couldn't tell which way that was. My mind had lost all control, leaving my body weak and near collapse from trying to fight the fear. My body trembled violently, sending the signal that the muscles couldn't support my frame much longer, but deep down I knew I wasn't going to crumble like a cookie; I was going to detonate like the atomic bomb. I could already feel my heart's hard, fast, relentless pounding in my head. I was about to explode - it was just a matter of time.

There was no way out of this and I knew it. Just stand and wait. The sound was getting louder; it would be here soon. A twig snapped. My head swung to the right. That's where it was, to the right. I knew now it was an animal. Its low guttural growl was now unmistakable. As it moved swiftly toward me, I got a brief look at the terror that threatened my life. It had the body of a man and the head of a beast. Its long protruding snout and razor sharp teeth dripped green, slimy saliva. Dark empty holes echoed where the eyes should be. Its breath was hot and carried the stench of death. As it knocked me to the ground, it began to laugh and started chewing on my hands. Screaming, and with what strength I had, I tried to stop the attack, but as I raised my arms all I could see were shards of bone, jutting out from raw, bloodied flesh where my hands had once been. With one last agonizing shriek...I woke up.

This nightmare happened as I neared the end of writing this book and it shook every amount of confidence I had that I could complete the effort. Did someone or something not want me to finish this book and keep a truth from being told or was it just cold feet? Admittedly, the end of the book was the most difficult for me to write because I didn't want to preach. I just wanted to present some compelling evidence to the reality of "life after death." I made several attempts at the last chapters and finally told my sister, Betty, I just couldn't do it. She gently reminded me how far we had come and that I couldn't give up now. We had over two years of incredible pictures and unique events that neither of us had asked for and they simply could not be dismissed as coincidental or insignificant. Through it all our lives have changed for the better.

The dead are dead, but that is not to say that death is the absolute end. Both Betty and I were raised with a Catholic background that reminded us all the time to "be good or else." We were taught that upon leaving this world, a person either went to Heaven or Hell, or for those not quite good enough, a stop-over in Purgatory might be in order before moving on. Hence, our firm belief in "life after death." We would one day be joined with those lost to us. Of course, we all hope that the reunion would take place in the positive of the three locations. But, is there another world responsible for the things that go "bump in the night," those eerie sounds that seem hard to pinpoint, or the glimpses of something from out the corner of the eye and odd smells from nowhere? Betty had always been open-minded about where these elusive possibilities originated, but I still needed logical and rational explanations to provide the level of comfort I required. This need was a defense mechanism, a system that was activated early in life.

I remember being alone in my big double bed and screaming with fear at the sounds coming from every corner in my bedroom. My mother would rush in to save me. Gently, she would say, "ghosts and monsters are not real." She would then systematically search my room, check my closet and tightly close its door and look under the bed. Each time proving to me that there was no reason to be afraid. Then she would give me a soothing kiss as she snugly tucked me in. With my protective barrier properly in place, I would fall asleep peacefully. No monster or ghost could get me under all those covers, especially if they were tucked in right! This became the foundation for my very adamant position on the many ghost stories I've heard throughout my life. There was no way I was going to believe that Grandma could come back and scare the living daylights out of me in the middle of the night. The dead are dead, BUT...then came the pictures.

Surrounding the pictures came a series of dreams and events that when combined together, began to tell a delightful story, laced with a bit of humor and a lot of love. Betty finally decided it was time to share our remarkable experiences, so with her constant encouragement and a promise to help, I began this book. Four times I started, four times I stopped and four times she prodded, pushed and nagged me until I started again. We are not professional photographers, nor are we life long seekers of the "unexplained." These events simply happened and the pictures were too dynamic to be folded into the pages of an album and left on a shelf.

We hope that you, too, will gain some fresh new insights and perspectives from our experiences.

God bless,
Linda and Betty

Linda, Pat & Betty
July, 1992

PROLOGUE
JULY, 1993

"Lynn?" Silence. I couldn't say it too loud. Standing in a cemetery to me was like standing in a church. Respect prevented me from yelling.

"Lynn?" I called again. "Damn, where'd she go?" I was standing alone in an old cemetery in Millegeville, Georgia, the original capital of that state until after the end of the Civil War, located about seventy-five miles southeast of its present capital, Atlanta. It was a huge burial ground with towering monuments. Many of these monuments had stood for nearly two hundred years giving testimony to the persons placed below their bases. It was easy to see how Lynn and I had gotten separated. We referred to this activity as "cemetery stomping." It was a way to stay connected, to remember and learn about the past. How had our cemetery stomping gotten started? My mind drifted to the time when it all began. That little getaway trip to Hinckley, Minnesota...

...Lynn and I had decided we needed a little vacation. Just two nights away from husbands and kids. The drive was a short one, only an hour and a half. We found a motel with a pool, critical to the relaxation we were looking for, got a bite to eat, and headed to the local casino with our allotted sixty dollars that we figured we could afford to lose. Big time gamblers we were not. Later that evening my brother, Pat, joined our outing.

By one o'clock in the morning, Lynn had lost her money. She decided to call it a night and go back to the motel, but I still had money left. I decided it was about time I learned to play Blackjack and Pat offered to coach me. He wasn't a pro, but he did understand the game. There was room for him to join the table, but he never played a hand. He was going to help his big sister, so he just stood next to me for five hours. What a great time we had. Pat had a hearty, contagious laugh and a manner about him that had the other players and even the dealer laughing most of the night. No other table in the casino had as much fun or attracted so much attention. At dawn we left, as I clutched the twenty dollars I had started with. He had been a good teacher, but we both knew not to look a gift horse in the mouth.

Later that morning after Pat left for home, Lynn and I went to tour this small town and visit the locally publicized fire museum. I just couldn't turn down the opportunity to explore historical events. Since I was a child, I had always wanted to be a history teacher, and this museum was going to help satisfy my need to know. The pictures and journals at the museum told a horrifying story. One hundred years ago a devastating fire had destroyed this part of Minnesota and many lives had been lost. A memorial had been erected in the local cemetery to honor them, so that became our next stop. We indeed found what had been described at the museum; three long burial trenches that could still be seen today as grass covered mounds. A plaque also helped identify the location. What a terrible loss of life. Walking through a cemetery was like walking through time, and to read a name on a headstone makes a lost life not so forgotten. No one should ever forget...

...So now, here I stood in this Georgia cemetery, minus my touring companion, neighbor and best friend of ten years, and it was getting dark. The massive trees were doing their best to block out what was left of the day's sun. This time, I found it a little uneasy standing among the dead because I was alone. I began to fidget and could feel a prickling sensation beginning just under my skin. "Damn nerves," I thought to myself. I always believed the dead were dead, so what was I so afraid of? Living through the 50s was the problem... "The Blob," "Godzilla," all the giant bugs that ate entire cities, squashing and unleashing their own brand of population control on the world. I would never forget what "House on Haunted Hill" had done to me. That "fine film" had given me nightmares for years. Ghosts creating mayhem and terror for people forced to spend the night in a creepy old house. Then, of course, there was the current avalanche of horror I read from Stephen King. The adrenaline rush I had gotten from these experiences was great, but now my imagination was running wild because, I wasn't just a watcher, a by-stander, I was a participant. "There's nothing to be afraid of," my mother's words replayed, but I really needed to find Lynn. Sure, it was interesting to both of us to know who the graveyard's inhabitants were, who had been there the longest, how old had they been when they passed on, but a strong fascination for historical events could not outweigh the fact that it was getting dark. The original "tour option" hadn't included me standing alone, in the dark, in a cemetery. I replayed in my mind what had brought me there...

The original reason for the trip to Georgia had been to get training on and bring back a computer. I was starting a home graphics business to compliment my brother's part-time business in garment printing. Brother and sister were going to work together and make some extra money: something we had both wanted to do for a long time. With training on the machine done for the day Lynn and I decided on some sightseeing. When we left the motel our mission had been a simple one: to drive to the old part of the city, take the walking tour, and view some old southern mansions. (My daughter Jennifer had come along on the trip as a third driver, but decided it was too hot and stayed behind.) That particular night in Georgia was just what you would imagine a southern night in the middle of summer to be, hot and humid. The air was still and oppressive and my skin felt sticky and dirty. I wasn't glowing, I was sweating! I was just sure no amount of soap and water would ever take the feeling away. No one walked the streets except for us, two northern girls who were wide eyed at the great mansions they were seeing. The only sounds to be heard were our footfalls and some strange noises coming from somewhere high in the trees. It sounded like a thirty pound grasshopper that I sure hoped wouldn't lose its footing and free-fall to the ground. Each time we stopped, so did the sound. We were being watched. From around a corner, a block in front of us came a little old lady. It surprised me that someone her age could tolerate such heat. Well, with age comes knowledge so, Lynn and I approached the woman to ask some questions. We explained our visit to her hometown and then asked about the strange noises.

"A huge Southern locust," the elderly woman answered with a gentle accent, and with no breath in between she asked, "Did you see our cemetery? It's very old and has some big, beautiful monuments in it." After getting directions, we planned that the local cemetery would be our next, and from the look of the sun's position, our last stop. We would have to hurry, but we had forgotten to ask her where the original Governor's Mansion was. That had been the priority on our tour, but when we turned around, the old woman was gone. Gone where? How could anyone that old move so fast, especially in this God forsaken heat? We both thought it was strange, but had no time to dwell on it. We had to get moving. The Governor's Mansion would have to be missed. It would be later, that I would wonder about a connection between the old woman, the cemetery and the mansion.

So now, just where the heck was Lynn...
...Many of those buried in this particular cemetery were in cement houses sitting above ground. One of the sites had its stone lid slid a few inches to one side. Was the person in there really above the ground? Was there a coffin in there or just a pile of bones on the dirt? I was scared, but distracted from the feeling by a driving curiosity. Deep inside I already knew, but seeing was truly believing.

"Lynn, there you are," I said with a sigh of relief. "Where have you been?"

"I got side tracked on the other side of the cemetery. We better get going, it's getting dark," Lynn answered.

"First, help me slide this slab over some more," I said struggling to move the lid. I was peeking through the open corner, but couldn't tell what was in that dark void. If I could just get the tomb open a little more.

"No way," Lynn replied "Are you crazy? You can't mess with the dead." I knew she was afraid. She believed in ghosts.

"All I want to know is if they really are sitting on top of the ground," I said, matter of factly. "I'm not going to disturb anything. Remember Lynn, the dead are dead."

"Listen," Lynn replied "Grave stomping and reading names is one thing, messing with that slab is another. NO!"

"If my *sister* were here, she would jump at the chance to help me," I coaxed.

I continued to try, but sometimes Lynn had no sense of adventure. I couldn't move the lid alone, so it would have to remain a mystery. I later regretted not thinking to put the camera into the opening, utilizing the flash to see what turned up on the picture.

The sun slipped a little more. Time to return to the safety of our motel, the comfort of air conditioning, and a cool drink. We got into the van and began making our way back. We drove slowly, trying to get one last eyeful before leaving this beautiful part of the city, when one very fine old building caught our eyes. It was the Old Governor's Mansion. We weren't going to miss it after all! Lynn drove around the block and parked on the far side of the street. Standing outside near the curb was a sign explaining what the building had been; the Governor's Mansion at the time Millegeville was the capital of Georgia, and identifying it as a National Historical Monument. While Lynn waited in the van, I jumped out to get a picture of the great old structure. I stood in the middle of the deserted street with the sun going down behind me and snapped the picture. It would be days later when a strange image on that photo would be discovered.

CHAPTER 1
THE "MOLLIE PICTURES"

"Talking of ghosts, it is wonderful that six thousand years have now elapsed since the creation of the world, and still it is undecided whether or not there has ever been an instance of the spirit of any person appearing after death. All argument is against it, but all belief is for it." Thus remarked the eighteenth-century English writer, Samuel Johnson, to his friend and biographer, James Boswell. "This is a question," he went on, "Whether in theology or philosophy, that is one of the most important that can come before the human understanding."

"Why are ghosts so fascinating?" researchers have asked through the ages and the answer becomes apparent: "Because they have always responded to some innate longing in human nature to pierce the veil which hides the future after death."

Peter Underwood, *Ghosts: And How to See Them,* Anaya Publishers Limited, 1993

It was a hot August day in 1993 and once again, like many times before, Betty, Pat, Jennifer and I were all gathered in my kitchen. We were discussing the two unusual pictures I had taken in Georgia. The picture of Lynn and Jennifer relaxing by the pool had what appeared to be a little fog to the left. The other had what I thought was a double exposure of a face off to the left; the image had an uncanny resemblance to Lynn. But, then I remembered that Lynn had remained in the van when I took the picture. It couldn't be her. So, just what *was* this stuff on my pictures? Jennifer and I were retelling our story of the events in Georgia, and how I came to take such strange pictures. "Boooo!...it must be a ghost," I finally laughed sarcastically, defense mechanism activated. Pat and Betty really gave us a hard time. Pat always believed that ghosts were the work of the

Old Governor's Mansion, July, 1993

Poolside, July, 1993

devil; while Betty, on the other hand, had always been fascinated with the idea. Neither one could believe that I, the skeptic would even lightheartedly consider the possibility of a ghost.

"Oh puh-lease," Betty blurted, "Since when do you believe in ghosts? This picture of fog next to the pool is someone's cigarette smoke!"

"No, I wasn't smoking. Look at the picture. No one is smoking," I answered. Pat just shook his head and told me I was nuts. Then I got THE LOOK! He had a way of placing the side of his index finger between his teeth, and making a surprised look of horror on his face. This was followed with a sarcastic snicker. I knew the instant he did this that, I was dead in the water. No matter what I said he wasn't going to take it seriously. He could be insufferable.

This pool-side picture was like nothing we had seen before. We discussed and analyzed it, but finally dismissed its importance because the mansion picture was so much more impressive to us. We focused our attention on that one.

"Linda," Betty suggested, "This is just a reflection through your windshield when you took the picture." I explained our respective positions at the time the picture was taken and we continued the discussion with what the image looked like to each of us. At first, Jennifer and I saw the full head of a woman, while Betty and Pat both saw the full *body* of a headless woman walking in front of the building. Most people who looked at the picture would quickly see either one or the other, but could see both when pointed out to them. Eventually, we all saw both images.

I took the picture and scanned it into my computer. I thought there might be a way to see it more clearly if I could get rid of the clutter. I cropped the section that contained the image which eliminated the part of the picture I didn't want. Next, I tried to separate the image from the trees. For one reason or another (computer not sophisticated enough or limited expertise) I wasn't successful. Someone had to be able to tell us what these strange images were on our pictures and how they got there. What had gone wrong? These pictures were challenging some of my long held beliefs. I needed to find an answer.

"Yeah, yeah Linda, you find out and let us know," Pat and Betty both teased. It was always two against one, in one combination or another. If we could get on each other's case, for whatever reason, the odd man out would jump on the attacking side and the two would relentlessly dig, prod and push the targeted sibling. Now, it was my turn to be the target. The attacks were rarely heated; most of the time, they were done with humor and fun. We enjoyed each other and knew each other well. No one ever crossed the line.

Lynn and I began our investigation with the University of Minnesota. The receptionist who answered the phone informed me that they no longer did that type of research and referred me to the Minneapolis Institute of Arts' director of photography. With a little juggling of work schedules, we were able to meet with the director on a Friday afternoon. The director, a tall, elderly man examined the photos and negatives, and discussed with us lighting, film, development, sun spots and chemicals and came to only one conclusion: what was on the pictures was *on* the negatives, therefore, the *camera* saw something that the eye couldn't. He assured us that there was no fault in the developing process nor a problem with the camera.

"Then what did we take a picture of?" I asked.

He chuckled, "Do you want me to tell you it's a ghost?"

"Not unless you think it is. We just want to know the truth," I answered. He didn't know what the truth was. He had exhausted every photographic explanation he could think of. He could say what it wasn't, but he could not tell us what it was. Despite how unique we all thought the mansion picture was, he found the pool side picture much more intriguing. The smoky appearance really baffled him. It would seem we had a mystery on our hands. The need for a logical explanation pushed me on. Was it a ghost? Heaven forbid!

This had all started in Georgia so I decided to continue our investigation there. I already knew from our visit that the Governor's Mansion had served as the state's capitol until just after the Civil War. After that time, it was used as the housing facility for the deans of the college adjacent to the site. More recently, the deans continue to occupy the upper floor, while the remainder is open to the public as a historic landmark.

I needed more details, so later that week I called the Mansion to ask more questions. I wanted to find out if anyone had been murdered in the Mansion or if there had been any unexplained deaths. After all, isn't that what ghosts are, unsettled spirits who can't rest because of violent actions at the time of their death? (That's always been my understanding.) The director told me she had been recently hired, and the major thrust of her job was to uncover the full story of the building and its residents. (The history of the Mansion and its occupants had never been thoroughly researched.) She had no specific information at that time, but she did tell me of a college student who had done his thesis on the Mansion. He insisted that it was haunted with the ghost of a cook or housekeeper who had lived there around 1850. The odd occurrences, he stated, included beds being turned down and the smell of food cooking in the kitchen when no one was in it. It was not known how she died, but her name was Mollie, so our pictures became known as the "Mollie Pictures." The director was interested in seeing the pictures and requested that I mail them to her. She said that she would keep in touch. Shortly after we ended our conversation, I decided not to mail the pictures because I was already thinking of a return trip.

In a follow-up call several months later, I was told that the progress of her research would be slow. The building was in need of major restoration and the focus of her job had shifted to funding for the project, so her historical research had been put on the back burner. She told me she was disappointed that I hadn't mailed the pictures to her because a local author, who at the time was working on a book about the ghosts of Georgia, said she was interested in our pictures and story. A missed opportunity! After ending the phone conversation, I reported my findings to Lynn. We sure weren't getting anywhere handling this long distance, so we re-discussed a second trip to Millegeville to dig up our own answers, but time and money stalled our investigation. For the next year and a half, there was not much talk of the "Mollie Pictures."

CHAPTER 2
"PASSING ON"

As they walked on conversing, a flaming chariot and flaming horses came between them, and Elijah went up to heaven in a whirlwind.

God, *The Holy Bible*, 2Kings 2:11

Three months later...

...When Pat entered the hospital that day in November 1993, the last thought Betty and I had was that we would have to make the decision to "let him go." We were no strangers to death, but that didn't make it any easier. Our mother died following an eight year illness, when Betty was eleven, Pat was sixteen and I was nineteen. Our father died twenty years after that on Christmas day, 1987. Being Irish, he had often times told us that when he passed on that no one was to cry; everyone was to party. Hence, we found ourselves gathering for our traditional "party" on the biggest holiday of the year, and, "up his nose" we cried anyway!

As devastating as these two major events had been, they did serve to tighten the bond between the three of us. Not a week passed without telephone calls to each other, poker and board game nights, night clubbing, barbecues, church gatherings, holiday dinners and just plain dinner, dinners. As we are all aware, life presents challenges and conflicts on a regular basis. The bond between the three of us grew strongest whenever one of us found ourself locked in one of these struggles. The three of us fought very hard to help each other get through the difficult times. One of Pat's most difficult times had been his divorce three years before. I figured the nightmare for him should have been over. But, a month before his death, he was enmeshed in another battle with his former wife and her new husband complicated matters even more. Pat's daughter, after spending the summer with her dad, had decided she wanted to live with him, so he found himself petitioning for custody and a reduction in his child support. A mediator was selected and a date set for a hearing. Pat's ex-wife's refusal to cooperate caused cancellation of the meeting just one day before, infuriating him. What should have been equitable for both parties was shot to hell because of her stubbornness. He was paying double for the needs of his daughter, but had to drop the issue because a long court battle would have been too costly. His only alternative was to try to reason with her. Betty and I were livid and tried to support him the best way we could.

To add to his problems, his girlfriend of three years had decided their relationship was over. She couldn't get Pat to commit to a permanent relationship. Oh, what a surprise! He still wasn't out of the first mess. It was heart-breaking for Betty and me to watch him struggle so hard. Pat and his new love had been very happy together. He had grown emotionally as well as spiritually, so when it ended, Pat was devastated. He couldn't understand why, especially with this battle raging with his ex, that his girlfriend would press him so hard. The past had taught him that he had to first get his life settled, before he could move on.

What Betty and I thought was an emotional depression caused by all these events was only part of it. A large part of his distress was actually a symptom indicating a problem with his heart. Pat was stuck in a vicious circle. These recent events were taking their toll on his heart, and this physical weakness was affecting his emotional well being. Even his doctor had failed to detect a heart problem and had, instead, prescribed anti-depressants. Betty and I spent hours on the phone with him and numerous visits were made to each of our homes. We encouraged him to "hang in there"... we knew it would get better. We reminded him that there had been "life" after his divorce and there would be "life" again. He simply responded, "why can't I see that?"

Prior to entering the hospital, Pat had complained of flu-like symptoms, heartburn, no appetite, and an upset stomach. Rachel, worried about her dad, called Betty from school to report his illness. That was early morning, the fifth of November. Betty phoned him immediately. Beside the information Rachel had given her, Pat also said he was experiencing chest pain but was convinced it was just a pulled muscle from being sick during the night. Betty insisted that he see a doctor and told him to get ready because she was on her way over to pick him up. She picked Rachel up from school and drove to his house. This early November morning found the roads slippery and covered with ice and snow, so the ten minute ride to the emergency room seemed to take an hour. Instead of being dropped off at the door, Pat demanded that Betty "just pull it around to that parking spot." He just had the flu...

...Immediately, Pat was descended upon by doctors, nurses and other emergency personnel who diagnosed his condition as critical. Betty called me at work. Fifteen minutes later, a nurse led Betty to that awful forbidden room where they tell you the bad news. Betty dreaded the words that came from the nurse's mouth, "your brother's heart has stopped. They're doing CPR right now. Would you like me to call clergy?" Once the words became real to her, Betty rushed to a phone and called me again. I left work immediately to join them. My mind was reeling. I prayed that I would get there in time. Thank God I had seen Pat just two days earlier. He had been especially upset that day, so when he had started to leave, I had given him a hug, told him I loved him and tried to reassure him everything would work out. I was glad to have been given that special gift for a final memory.

Damn Minnesota weather; I didn't make it before Pat went into surgery. Betty told me that once Pat had been stabilized, they had rushed him in for heart by-pass. The intense look on the faces of the medical team surrounding Pat's cart spoke of the urgency of the situation. In their hurriedness they did stop, though momentarily, for Betty to take his hand and kiss his blue forehead. Fear gripped her by the throat as optimism for his recovery began slipping away. The next five days would prove the enormous strength of the human spirit, fueled only by the hand of God, who "tops off the tank" with the endurance necessary to handle such demanding times. As Pat fought for life, Betty and I were constantly being yanked into what seemed like a million emotional directions all at one time.

The surgery was as successful as it could have been, but the damage to Pat's heart was significant and his brain showed little activity. The doctors were not very hopeful, but they said Pat was young and strong so, just maybe, he would beat the odds. Those who should have been waiting for Pat to emerge from his coma were his sisters, his children, and close family and friends, but this situation had gotten much more complicated. The possibility of the death of a loved one is hard enough to handle, but Betty and I also found ourselves needing to deal with the presence of Pat's ex-wife and her husband, ex-in-laws, and Pat's ex-girlfriend. This montage of people left us struggling with right and wrong. Do we allow all these people access to Pat's intensive care room? We couldn't understand what brought these people here? Was it concern for Pat and his family? How about guilt? I was walking the edge. With both parents deceased and being the oldest in the family, I was feeling the enormous weight of responsibility. Not only for Betty and I, but for Pat as well.

Finally, a nurse approached me asking, "Who are all these people?"

"Isn't it amazing what imminent death brings out of the woodwork," I answered. With mounting tension and frustration in my voice, I finished my run-down of this enormous cast of characters. She lovingly took my hand and told me no matter how difficult it was, I had to take control of the situation. That was all the reassurance I needed. From that point on, what I believed Pat's wishes to be would come first. No one was allowed into his room unless Betty or I approved it.

Life and death decisions are the hardest to make and now we were faced with one of those controversial choices. Pat wasn't getting better. Should we turn off his life support machines and "let him go?" Anne, a friend of Betty's had reminded her of the power of the Scapular, a one inch by one and a half inch cloth rectangle attached by a cord and worn around the neck and the medal of St. Jude, the patron saint of the hopeless or lost. Both are long time traditions in the Catholic church that provide protection and special blessings to those who are ill and to those who are dying. Anne had purchased these items for Betty the night before because the following day, November ninth, was determined to be the day to make the final decision. Betty entered the hospital very early clutching the scapular and the medal, and urgently looked for a priest to bless them before she pinned them on Pat. The only person to be found was a Lutheran minister. Catholic or not, at this point it didn't matter. Betty went directly to his room. As she attached the blessed items to his gown, she leaned over and whispered, "This is it Pat. This is your chance to knock their socks off. You show them!"

I guess I had always known from the first day of Pat's illness that it would eventually come to that decision, but once again, circumstances would make it even harder than it had to be. At the hospital, we found ourselves gathered in a big conference room. Betty and I and our families, Pat's children, our step-mother, our aunt and, to my shock, his ex-wife and her husband met to discuss Pat's treatment. As calmly as I could, I asked the two of them to leave. I deferred to her response that she was there for her children, but said that her husband had to go! She began screaming at me in an attempt to rationalize his presence. I exploded in a flood of uncontrollable tears as the week and all of its twisted events caught up to me. The priest I had called to the meeting, Father Reiser, a long-time friend and employer for the last seventeen years, grabbed me so that I wouldn't end up in a heap on the floor. As Betty rushed to my side, her husband Craig, stood and told Pat's ex-wife's husband, "You don't belong here, get out!" He finally left.

Once tension eased, the meeting started. By that time, the group had grown to include three doctors and the head nurse. They began by discussing Pat's current physical condition. It was true; Pat had no brain activity. During the night they had turned down the machines a little to see his response, his vital signs dropped immediately. The machines were simply keeping his body functioning. Father Reiser solidly backed their findings and added that "if it were my brother, I would let him go." What everyone in the room had to say was important, but the final decision rested solely with Betty, Pat's two children and me. We had to retake our places in this out-of-control nightmare, so in turn, one by one, I asked each of his children and Betty if they understood what the doctors had said. I knew that we would all have to live with the decision, so any reservations had to be talked about at that time. After much discussion, we agreed to turn off the machines. Slowly and quietly, we all returned to Pat's room.

Circling the bed, we listened while Father Reiser gave Pat "Last Rites" as the machines went silent. We waited the few minutes it should have taken for Pat to pass on. Father blessed him, read a prayer, glanced at the monitor, returned to his Bible, and blessed him again. What should have taken only a few minutes, didn't. The nurses brought us chairs and arranged them theater-style alongside Pat. This was crazy! I almost expected them to bring popcorn next. We waited...and waited. The only interruption was the priest excusing himself to go and move his car from its no parking space. This was taking longer than he expected...longer than any of us expected. He assured me he would return quickly.

When Father Reiser got back, Pat was still holding his own, so he blessed him again. The doctors were amazed and found it necessary to call a second meeting to discuss a new concern: Pat wasn't passing on, and if he was going to live, he had to be returned to surgery to remove the pump that assisted his heart and would eventually hinder his recovery. His condition was fragile, so the doctors were sure he would not survive the procedure. Well, survive he did! Not only were we shocked, but the doctors were astounded. "Do you suppose, Linda, we have a miracle happening because of the scapular and the medal?" Betty asked.

"I have no idea what to think for sure," I answered.

"You know Linda, Pat and I had only a month ago talked about how awful it would be to lay dying in a hospital bed with your family standing around waiting for your expiration. Do you suppose that's why things are happening like this?"

"All I know for sure is I'm exhausted," I answered. What I didn't tell anyone at the time was how scared I was that Pat's newly repaired heart would pump forever, and with no brain activity, the rest of his life would be spent in a nursing home. I was so tired. God would have to carry this one for me.

"Well it's for sure that he's knocking everyone's socks off," Betty said as we all walked to the elevator with guarded optimism. It was time to go home.

Around 5:30 a.m. on the tenth of November, a nurse called to say that Pat had died. It was over; it was time to make funeral arrangements. Thirty minutes later, the nurse called to say that he was "back." What did she mean back? He was still alive! Then an hour later, she called and said that Pat had "passed on" again! The distress in her voice was evident as she tried to apologize for what she thought must appear to be incompetence. "Are you sure this time?" I asked her in tears. I couldn't take much more of this. She was sure, so I reminded her of our decision to donate his eyes. (Several months later, Betty and I were told of surgeries successfully bringing sight to two people.) Now came the preparations for the funeral.

At the service, the priest said to the gathering, "I think we blessed him to death." Betty and I smiled at each other while I remembered something Pat had said to me two weeks earlier: "Linda," he said, "Pray for me, because I don't know where I'll be." Well, we had indeed prayed for him; he had provided us with no choice and we continue to do so.

We buried him in a small cemetery ...a quiet, peaceful, pretty little cemetery. His life with us was over. Or was it?

CHAPTER 3
STRANGE OCCURRENCES

As long as there have been human beings, people have claimed experiences with phenomena that, according to the prevailing religious or scientific orthodoxy, were not supposed to exist.

Jerome Clark, *OMNI*, February 1987

Once a loved one has been laid to rest the hard part comes, going on without them. Having lived on after losing my parents, I knew I would survive losing Pat. Time would lessen the hurt, but adjusting to the loss of a sibling felt different. I would need to sort through the unfamiliar feelings.

I found myself not having much time to grieve. Immediately following Pat's death, I was thrust into paperwork. There had been no will, so I was appointed by the court to be the executor of his estate. There was life insurance to request, bills to pay, a house and cars to sell, taxes to file, two dependent teenagers to be taken care of. To top it off, his ex-wife who fought me every step of the way. When the pressure would get too intense, I would go to the cemetery. One time, at one o'clock in the morning, in the rain, with a beer in one hand, a box of tissue in the other and sobbing, I stomped all over his grave. With no sod on the site and the dirt soggy, I was proud of the big dents I was making. I was so angry! How dare he die, denying Betty and me his presence and especially, leaving me with such a big mess. One other thing bothered me; he now had the answers to life and death; something Pat and I had debated endlessly before he died. In a twisted sort of way, it seemed he had the upper hand. Dying wasn't the hard part, *living* was the hard part, and dealing with the anger was the hardest part of all. So, instead of grieving a little at a time, I did it in huge bursts.

The obstacles seemed insurmountable, but by the grace of God, I found a lawyer who was truly an angel. Pat's estate was small, but she agreed to partial payment and worked "pro bono" for the remainder. Little by little (How do you eat an elephant? One bite at a time!) with her help, I began the task of settling his affairs. My first priority had to be toward Pat's children and Pat's life insurance money, which needed to be placed in a trust for them. With his ex-wife already having two lawyers, one for the children and one for herself (retained before Pat even died!) she had a jump on me. She had filed for and received Pat's life insurance money. Pat had failed to take her name off as beneficiary, although the divorce document had removed her as such.

My second priority was the selling of his house. Three times prior to his death he tried unsuccessfully to sell his home. The problem was he wanted too much for it; I never thought he really wanted to sell it. The court told me to act quickly, to price it right, and sell it fast. The realtor I selected to list his house was a long-time family friend. He suggested we start with a high asking price, giving us room for negotiating at the time of an offer. I was hesitant to agree, but conceded to his experience. I would give it a little time.

Then came the matter of Pat's cars. His prize possession had been his Monte Carlo SS. After getting several value estimates, Betty and Craig bought the car from the estate. The sale of the second car was to be (oh, what a surprise!) more complicated. Because no funds were available to maintain any payments, the court instructed me to call the creditors, explain the situation and buy time to increase the estate's assets with the sale of these larger items, enabling me to clear his debts. The bank holding the paper on this second car seemed cooperative in the beginning, but then turned ugly. One afternoon, with no warning, they came and towed the car away. When my aunt, who had lived with Pat called and told me the car had been stolen, I was livid! I just knew the bank had repossessed it. I got little "Miss Bank, Blood-Sucking, Cold-Hearted, I-Got-The-Power-and-You-Don't" on the phone. I had tried hard to work with the bank, so I couldn't understand this sudden turn. Her attitude was heartless, and I got no where with her; she said the car would be sold at an auction, and they would send me the bill for any money left on the loan. Auctions never bring enough money to cover a loan. My heart sank. The estate was already in a position of default and simply couldn't sustain another bill. With the sale of the Monte Carlo, I at least knew the estate would be able to pay the funeral expenses I had incurred. As far as the bank sending me a bill for the balance, I told her that I suspected there would be a snow storm in Hell before she saw a dime. I was overwhelmed! Betty did what she could to help, but again the weight of responsibility was enormous, and I felt very alone. I needed help and then...

...One night, I was awakened by the sound of someone coming up the stairs toward my bedroom and eventually coming to stand at my husband's side of the bed. Thinking our youngest son, Tom, was sick, I lay very still and waited for my husband to deal with him. (Ron was always better at handling the kids when they were sick; my stomach couldn't take it.) I lay there pretending to be asleep for what seemed a long time. Why wasn't Tom saying something? The silence scared me; maybe it wasn't Tom. I wanted to know who it was, but my increasing fear kept me from asking the simple question. In the dark at three in the morning, all I could see was the outline of someone wearing what appeared to be a white T-shirt. Soon it was pushing on our bed. One-two-three times. Our waterbed mattress didn't move. I should have felt something. The form then turned, and in continued silence, left the room. Once in the hallway, there was a bright flash and it was gone. The event had lasted just a couple of minutes.

I lay there for a minute or two longer trying to decide if I could even get out of bed. Terrified or not, I had to use the bathroom and I knew I would also have to go downstairs and be sure everything was okay. *Get a grip Linda*, I thought, *there's nothing to be afraid of.* Boy, how many times have I heard that since I was a kid. Now I was the adult who should know better. Slowly, I got out of bed, listened and then rushed to the bathroom and locked the door. With my heart pounding, *th-thump, th-thump*, I remembered how easy it had been for Jack Nicholson to axe his way through a bathroom door in "The Shining." There was no way I was safe in there. Once again the voice in my head tried to bring me back. *Get a grip,* it repeated. My heart pounded out its two cents of advice, *th-thump, th-thump*, stay right where you are. This wasn't healthy; I had to do something. Cautiously, I opened the door and stepped into the hall.

I stood at the top of the stairs for a minute with the light on, trying to hear any movement coming from down stairs. *Get a grip! Th-thump, th-thump!* I had to get some control. I took a couple of deep breaths and stiff legged, slowly inched my way down each step, trying to avoid the ones I knew creaked. It seemed to take forever to go down the fourteen stairs but, I suppose it's understandable when your knees won't bend. At the bottom, I turned to the right toward Tom's room and quietly opened his door. He was tangled in the bed sheets as though he had not been out of them for hours. *Get a grip!* One by one, I turned on every light in the living room to check the door and windows. I did the same in the kitchen and the mud room. *Th-thump, th-thump!* I had to remember to breathe. Everything seemed to be fine. So what had I experienced? I would double-check with Tom in the morning to see if he had been roaming the house during the night. It had to have been Tom. My body was starting to relax so, I went back to bed and tried to forget; I really needed some sleep.

The next morning I asked Tom if he had been up during the night carrying his flashlight. "No Mom, I wasn't up last night." he said, "And besides, the batteries in my flashlight have been dead for months." Goose bumps tingled on my arms. Next, I needed to check with my husband. "Ron, did I hear Tom come into our room last night?"

"No," he answered. "You must have been dreaming." I was sure I hadn't been dreaming, but my skeptical side would not allow any other explanation. Yet, the following events would begin to tug at what I thought was a well-rooted philosophy.

The listing on the house appeared first on a Sunday in February, 1994. Three days later, a full price offer came to us from a pre-approved buyer, who asked that nothing additional be done to close the deal. Ironically, this man lived just across the alley from Pat and had been looking for a house in the neighborhood for almost a year. He was divorced, like Pat, left handed, like Pat, and had a daughter the same age as Pat's. Did Pat have something to do with this? Then I rationalized, "right buyer, right time." I signed the sale agreement and the closing was set for thirty days later. *Push number one?*

The only way to secure the life insurance money was for me to make a motion to be the conservator for the children and to have trust funds set up for them. If someone had not made a move in that direction, there would soon be nothing left. When our day in court came, my attorney presented our position. She told the judge that what I really wanted was for the court to appoint a neutral party to be the conservator. Pat's ex-wife was asking that her brother be appointed. The court had ruled in our favor, and the judge stated, "Somehow I don't think that Pat would want his ex-wife's brother as conservator for his children!" Case closed! I felt bad, however, that his ex-wife had managed to spend thousands of dollars before I could legally have it taken from her. *Push number two?*

A few months, later to my amazement, a check from the bank

came in the mail. The car had sold for more than the estate owed on it! *Push number THREE?* These events brought back my question: had Pat been in my bedroom that night? I filed these strange events in my mind, but not too deep; something strange was going on and I figured I might have to develop a thought! The dead are dead! As always, logic had to prevail.

Amid all this, other unexplained things were also happening. One day in early April, Betty called me on the telephone. "Linda, the strangest thing just happened! I was cleaning in the kitchen after dinner and became overwhelmed with the smell of a man's cologne!"

"So," I said, "what's the big deal?"

"The big deal is, no one was in the kitchen with me," she answered. "It lasted for a few seconds and just disappeared." I told her, "The mind is a powerful thing. If it wants your nose to smell something it will." She insisted it wasn't in her head. I poo-pooed her and moved on with our conversation. I just knew she thought we had both been visited by Pat and for a fact, I wasn't going to get sucked into that. There was no way I was going to think that the dead could hang around. In my opinion, people who persisted in believing that their loved ones were still around were people who wouldn't or couldn't "let go." Betty is my little sister, so big sister, Linda would have to see to it that she didn't get trapped into denial. Oddly enough, this incident with the cologne wasn't going to be the last, nor was it going to be an exclusive event for Betty.

Shortly following the cologne smell, Betty called me again. This time her house was shaking. "Linda, this is too weird. This is the third day in a row that the kitchen and dining area of our house rumbled and at 5:24 pm!" She went on to describe the unusual sound. Although she had never been in an earthquake, she imagined the sound to be similar, the same sound heard when two mighty pieces of earth grind against each other. She couldn't feel any vibrations, but she expected at any time the floor would split and swallow them up.

"Did Craig have something running in your garage, like his air compressor?" I asked, knowing that her dining area and garage shared a common wall.

"No, I ran from that wall back over to the kitchen area and the sound was the same there. I thought about our plumbing, but Craig assured me it's not the pipes. Plus, Linda, three days in a row *at the same time*? The only thing I can think of is that Pat used to stop by a lot at that time, because he knew we would always be home. I don't know, Linda. What do you think?" I had absolutely no idea other than that was around the time Pat *first* died, even though it was afternoon not morning. I was just glad it wasn't my house; I'd had enough crap to deal with. The mystery was never solved; the shaking has never happened again.

Then Betty's ten year old daughter, Laura, had this experience...
...One spring afternoon, I was sitting on the living room floor playing a video game. Behind me was a bag like the ones you can get from a department store. It had handles. All of a sudden, I heard the bag rattle and when I turned around, the bag fell over and began rolling past me on its side. I watched it go around the corner of the living room, go down the hall and then go around another corner into my mom's bedroom. I was shocked and scared, but curiosity got me to go into my mom's room and there I found the bag. It was sitting upright, next to my mom's night stand. My mom and dad at the time were outside, talking in the driveway. My brother was gone too. Scared that I was alone, I ran out the door in my socks. Thank God, it wasn't winter. In a panic, I told my mom what happened...

...When Betty went inside to check on Laura's story, she found that the bag had indeed ended up in her bedroom and Laura assured her it had done so under its own power. But, just whose power had it been? Several odd facts about the episode; first...the bag had earlier contained some items concerning Pat's estate; second...it had ended up by Betty's night stand where she kept a notebook of thoughts that would later become her book called, "Is it a Bird, Is it a Plane, No It's Pat;" and third it happened at approximately 5:30 in the afternoon around the same time of day as the house shaking! Then several months later...

...October...it was going to be a long winter. During one of Minnesota's early snow storms, I found myself driving into Minneapolis to deliver an order of work uniforms to Curran's Restaurant. This had been Pat's favorite place to eat and happened to be managed by one of his long time high school friends, Dennis, now one of my best customers. Whenever I would make one these deliveries, I usually met Betty for lunch. After a hearty *hotdish* we asked the waitress to bring our checks. We hated to eat and run, but Betty had to get back to work and I had a long drive in crummy weather so, just one more quick cup of coffee. When we went to pick up our checks, what we thought was two turned out to be only one. Betty's wasn't there. We both searched the table, the floor, the outside and inside of her purse and mine. It was nowhere to be found. "Well it's not stuck to anything so, this must be a 'Betty day.' Mine is free!" Betty said with a sly smile.

When we got up to the register, Betty told the cashier that she never received her bill. The waitress over heard and came over to the counter.

"I am sure I set it on the table," she said. She returned to the table and quickly checked to see if we had missed it and then looked in the pocket of her apron where she kept her checks before giving them to customers. It was nowhere to be found, so Dennis figured the amount on his adding machine. Betty settled up and we left.

Three days later, her husband Craig came into the kitchen carrying a restaurant check in his hand. "What's this?" he asked and laid it on the counter. Betty looked down in total amazement.

"That's my bill for the lunch I had three days ago with Linda, but they never gave me a check. Where did you get it?" she asked.

"It was lying on the front seat of your car and you never saw it?" he asked her.

"Craig, that check WAS NOT there before. Don't you think I would have noticed an eight inch by five inch piece of heavy weight paper in the front seat of the car? Just how could it appear suddenly for you three days later? And look, its not dirty or bent in any way!" she told him. Craig had no idea. Betty called me with her story, and I had to admit I had no idea what to think of the whole situation either. I had followed her out of the restaurant and was sure it hadn't been stuck to her butt or anything else for that matter. It was too big to miss. I would have seen it. And another thing, she had danced around her car for five minutes brushing off the snow so, unless it were held to her by super glue, it certainly would have fallen to the ground. So, we had another little mystery; how had it gotten in her car?

CHAPTER 4
DREAMS
By Betty

Our unconscious does know more than we know. It is as if the unconscious is expanded into outer nature and has information which we cannot have. Therefore in dreams you sometimes get warnings or information about things you cannot possibly know.

VonFranz, Marie-Louise, *The Way of the Dream*, Shambhala Publications, 1992

Betty's dreams will be told by her...

...In my first dream, following Pat's death, I found myself in his living room giving him a hug and telling him I loved and missed him. He told me to sit on his couch so I could see clearly the board he had propped on an easel. He then began to enlighten me with what happened to the soul after you die. This would be so typical of Pat to do. Many times he would stop over for a soda on any given evening, and we would speculate and share our thoughts on God and religion. Often the clock would read one in the morning even though we both had to work the next day. So here he was, earnestly explaining how after death the soul would be lit up as a small bright light and would be found high up on his board. In one area, toward the top, there was no light. Pointing, he told me that the light was missing because someone we both had known well had had an abortion. I could tell by his demeanor that this bothered him. Having your soul lit was of the utmost importance and our ultimate goal, Pat had explained.

When I woke up, I was anxious to call Linda. After telling her in detail about the soul's continued existence, I went on to tell her about the abortion. She reminded me that the woman Pat mentioned in the dream had experienced a miscarriage years before. At least, that is what we were told. But Pat had stressed specifically that it was an abortion. Days later and after sharing the dream with others, "light" was shed on the deep, dark secret. This woman had indeed had an abortion. Could it be that Pat revealed the "secret" as proof that he, in a sense, was still with us? Is it possible that in our deepest sleep, doors are opened to allow this type of communication to take place; when in our conscious state of mind, these doors become locked?

Approximately seven months had gone by since I'd had one of "those" dreams again. Even when I did experience it, it seemed insignificant and I was not going to even mention it to anyone. This certainly would have been out of character for me, so, over lunch a couple days later with Linda, I told her my dream...

...Pat and I were lead singers in a rock band (something the two of us had joked about many times) and were performing for a small group down by a lake. Pat was holding the microphone for me, but this was posing a problem. He held it so close to my mouth, that my lips kept hitting the microphone. When the band took its break, I took the opportunity to tell him to stop jamming the mike right into my mouth. He politely agreed, but we never did get a chance to start the second set...the dream was over. Linda was not too impressed, nor was I for that matter, until three days later. August 15, 1994, Linda's birthday.

We held a small birthday party for Linda at the club where we would gather every Friday for country line dancing and to release our week's stresses with friends. A friend of ours was playing in the band that evening, so my plan for Linda was to have him sing her a song. Not just the traditional birthday song, but one I had found on a greeting card. He had agreed, but what I didn't know was that he wanted me on stage to sing and he would accompany me on the guitar. I was horrified! I had always thought singing on stage would be fun, but now it was to be a reality and that certainly gave me a whole different view of my fantasy! Me on stage in front of people singing? After much prompting, I finally joined him on stage. The crowd was only a blur. Well, at least I didn't have to try to picture them all in their underwear! He handed me the microphone and said, "Hold it right up to your mouth. Get it right up to your mouth." I had been hit with some major deja vu....MY DREAM! Could this really be happening? I started singing timidly while he strummed his guitar. He was so good at ad-libbing. By the time I got to the end, I thought I sounded pretty good! When he joined us during his break, I asked him why he told me to hold the microphone so close. His reply, "Lead singers always sing close and backup singers hold it further away." So that's why the microphone had to be close to my mouth. Not having any knowledge of this only made my dream more phenomenal.

Once again, I found myself experiencing something that I first realized in a dream. This had never happened to me before and I started to question why it was happening now. Although, it was strange; it was also wonderful...literally a dream come true. The impact that it had on Linda was surprising too. She said she felt as though Pat and I were together, wishing her a happy birthday like we had done so many times in the past and how truly special my singing gift had been to her. She smiled. I could also imagine in my mind Pat's "index finger" going up to his mouth and faintly hear his hearty laugh.

CHAPTER 5
PSYCHIC INTERPRETATION

***PSYCHIC**...Any individual who is sensitive to phenomena beyond the five senses and aware of activity in the ethereal dimension. Psychics can often see spirit forms, hear spirit voices, and "know" events that are going to happen in the future. It is important to recognize the difference between this natural gift and mental illness.*

Hazel M. Denning, Ph.D. *True Hauntings*,
Llewellyn Publishing, 1996

Going to work one morning, Betty, was listening to a radio station that "plays more music than anyone else." Their guest that week was a psychic who came to Minneapolis from time to time to do readings for the locals. "That's the answer," she said to herself. "Linda and I will make an appointment." She ran this by me and believe it or not, I was willing to give it a try. Seeing a psychic was something I never imagined myself doing. I believed them to be frauds preying on the weaknesses of distraught people, but we certainly had strange things happening and two suspicious pictures. Maybe it was time for me to explore this option; it couldn't hurt.

The appointment was for a Friday afternoon. I have to admit I was a little excited about seeing a psychic. What if we really could get some answers? Jennifer and I met Betty at her house, and then drove to a hotel located in Bloomington, a southern suburb of Minneapolis. The instructions we had to follow were: only one person could go in; we had to pay ninety dollars in cash, and no tape recorder would be allowed. I should have seen it coming. The plan was as follows: I would be the one to go in, more logical, more skeptical and less emotional than Betty; Jennifer and Betty were to wait in the hallway with a tape recorder in hand, ready to turn it on when the appointment was over. They wanted me to tell them everything that was said, and get it on tape, so I would not forget anything.

We all waited nervously out in the hallway. When it was my turn, a secretary collected our ninety dollars cash and I was ushered into one of the hotel's suites. "Suite" overstates it; it was just an ordinary hotel room. To the left as I entered were two double beds and sitting on the far side by the window, with its room darkening shade drawn, sitting in low light, was the psychic. She was middle aged, and finely dressed. Her silver gray hair was piled high on her head. Her hands were weighted down with enormous rings that I later decided had come from the hard earned money of many Midwesterners that, like myself, had been sucked in. There was a chair for me to sit in directly across from her, with a small table between us. "Sit down my dear," she said and our half hour began.

The first few things she told me, were the *only* things she told me that couldn't be disputed, because how could they be verified? I had a purple aura (not bad, I like purple); I am on a spiritual level of nine, ten being the highest (that's cool); and I possess psychic ability and should develop it (at ninety dollars per half hour, I guess so). I thought all of that was well and good, but I wasn't there for generalities, I was there to get some answers, so I started in.

I began by showing her the "Mollie Pictures." "Can you tell me who is in these pictures and why?" I asked.

"Well, my dear," she responded, "It is the spirit of a man, and it's obvious he liked trees and bushes because that's why his image appears there." First question asked and already I was in trouble.

(I had decided before I got to the meeting that I would offer no information that would tip her off, but these people have a clever way of finding out things you don't want them to know. Now this is where I messed up. Before I knew it, I had already told her my brother had passed away.) If she were truly psychic, *I* expected her to tell me things no one else but *I* could know.

Then I asked, "Who was my night visitor and why did he or she push on my bed three times? We have had many other strange occurrences that involve the number three. Does the number three mean anything significant?"

"Well, my dear," she said "It must have been Pat and the three pushes made on the bed was to let you know that he is on a spiritual level of three. He still has work to do." Beside giving me a feeble response, I had decided that she better not call me "dear" one more time.

"Will my brother's estate be settled favorably for his children?" I asked. At this time, not all the issues with his estate had been settled yet.

"Yes," she answered, "The will should take care of all that."

"But he didn't have a will," I said.

"Well, honey, there will be problems, but it will be very expensive if you get lawyers involved," was her off-handed reply and that was all she intended to say on the matter. She sure wasn't telling me something I didn't already know, but at least she hadn't called me dear. "Was she psychic?" I thought to myself sarcastically. My anger level was rising.

"Will my sister and I ever live together, like our two aunts did?" I asked. This was to humor Betty. I am still not real sure what we wanted to accomplish by asking this question. It certainty wasn't to help bring credibility to this reading, as no one can know if a prediction of the future is accurate or not, but I asked anyway.

"Do you and your sister get along?" the all-knowing psychic asked. "We did until now," I thought to myself. When I got out of there I was going to kill her, but one more question.

"Will my graphics business succeed?" I asked.

"Do you advertise?" she asked back. That was it. I was

on my way to the door.

As I stepped into the hallway and was speed-walking to the elevator, I heard Betty say to Jennifer, "Turn on the recorder!" As I fidgeted, waiting for my escape route, Jennifer shoved the recorder into my face. "Mom's encounter with the weird," she began taping.

"Turn that thing off! I can't believe I fell for this!" I said, feeling dumber than I had ever felt in my life and by God it was Betty's fault. We would speak about this.

"What? What did she say? Start from the beginning." Betty prodded.

The three of us left the hotel with an agreement that no one would ever know about our meeting with a psychic; though hours later at our weekly Friday night gathering, we would laugh about the experience with family and friends.

CHAPTER 6
"IT"...CAME FROM THE COMPUTER!
By Rachel

Since telephones are simple electrical devices, some of our deceased loved ones can seemingly manipulate electrical energy to achieve this type of communication. Other people described receiving messages on their telephone answering machines, pagers, tape recorders, radios, televisions, or COMPUTERS.

Bill and Judy Guggenheim, *Hello From Heaven!*,
Bantam Books, 1997

In the fall of 1994, Rachel, Pat's daughter called me about an experience she had in her car; a 1988 Oldsmobile Cutlass Sierra.

Rachel's story will be told by her...

...I went to pick up my brother Jared from a friend's house in Forest Lake. It was a crisp, clear evening, and the road conditions were great. Driving can be relaxing. The highway to and from took us past the house we used to live in before dad died. He would pick us up and drop us off from our weekend visitations. As I drove past on my way to get Jared, I had a strange feeling that dad was close by. It felt like more than just a memory produced by seeing the house; it felt as though he was sitting next to me. I dismissed the feeling as I reached the friend's house and Jared got in my car.

On our way home, the computer which is located in the middle of the dash board started to run amok! Its purpose is to display messages like: good morning, low fuel, change oil now. Each time a new message appears the machine sounds out a beeping tone to alert the driver. For fifteen minutes the screen flashed the following beginning with:

Beep...CHANGE OIL NOW...Beep, Beep
Then it went blank.
Beep...CHANGE OIL NOW...Beep, Beep.
Again it went blank.

The computer was constantly flashing one screen after another and continuously beeping. Figuring another thing had gone wrong with my car, I was getting angry and banged it a couple of times trying to get it to stop. I was sure it was a loose wire. While I continued to drive, Jared reported to me what the computer was saying. Thank God he was there. I was able to keep my eyes on the road and had someone to verify that I wasn't going nuts; the computer was. We were both starting to get a little freaked out. The next thing we saw on the screen is what I can best describe as looking like Chinese writing. Then...

Beep... L ...Beep, Beep.
Beep... O ...Beep.
Beep... V ...Beep.
Beep... E ...Flashing and Beeping
and then blank.
LOVE ...Constant Beeping.....
DECEMBER 31, 1999 ...Beep.
Beep... OR ...Beep.
Beep... GOD ...Beep....

"What the heck," I said to Jared. "What is going on with my computer?"

"Man, I don't know!" Jared answered stunned.

As I continued to drive Jared said that the computer repeated the same sequence: The strange writing, the word 'love' spelled out one letter at a time and then all together, the date, 'or,' and 'God.' I thought about pulling over to the side of the road and stopping, but it didn't seem like we were in any danger. Then the message changed a bit:

Scanning...Strange writing...Beep, then blank.

JG ...Flashing and Beeping

"Rachel, those are my initials!" Jared blurted.

Beep... LOVE ...Beep...........

The activity was beginning to slow down, so a couple of times I thought it might have gone dead. But then it would spring back to life, and start to repeat 'DECEMBER 31, 1999' and 'OR GOD'. After beeping and going blank, the next thing to appear on the screen was...

41 ...Blank, silence.

"Jared, the number 41. That's how old dad was when he died!"

As I pulled into the parking lot of our apartment and shut the car off, I thought there has to be a rational explanation for this, so I started the car up again and the computer did nothing. No beeps. No flashes. Nothing. I couldn't believe it. So what was it all about? I remember how my dad was always interested in the study of the Book of Revelation in the Bible and the end of the world, so was "December 31, 1999 Or God" a warning message? Or is this message along with the number "41" a way to identify that it was a communication from my dad? Nevertheless, Jared and I feel as though we received a letter signed...*From, Dad.*

The next morning I went out expecting the unit to be dead, but instead I was greeted with "Good Morning." I called General

Motors and questioned them about the event. They had never heard of a computer acting in that manner. Nearly two years have gone by, and the computer never malfunctioned again.

CHAPTER 7
THE "BLUE FOG"

He was purposeful in life so, is it possible...

He still wasn't sure he liked where he was, but knew there was nothing he could do about it. He had waited for a year. Family and friends had stopped from time to time to pay their respects and say a little prayer, but the opportunity had still not presented itself. Sure, he had dropped some subtle hints but knew that if he had a shot at all, it would be with Betty. She was much more receptive to these things then Linda. Linda's skepticism caused her to be much too bullheaded. The dead were dead. If she gave him just half a chance, he was in a position now to show her some of the truth. How many times had they discussed the possibilities of the reason for life and what follows? Now he knew, and Betty would have to help him unlock the door. The two dreams had been clever ideas. First, he would tell Betty something she could in no way know to be true. Everyone believed it had been a miscarriage; Betty would know the truth several days later and remember her dream. The second dream would be her singing on stage, he had always known how important that had been to her. With Linda's birthday coming, he had the perfect window of opportunity. Betty would not be able to dismiss either of these signs and she would remember and wonder. For a backup, just in case, there would be the cologne smells. Smells could leave a lasting impression and had been long since identified with those attempting to make themselves known to the living. Betty would not be sure, but she would not forget.

The most frustrating part of this whole "crossing over" experience was the inability to clearly get a message to those left behind. He remembered how close the three of them had been in life; there was no reason they should be distanced in death. He would have to be patient. That would be hard for him because he had never been very patient in life. His next plan he knew would be a sure thing. Linda would remember the "Mollie Pictures." She would remember the first time she was just a little swayed into believing in contact from the "other side." Seeing is believing.

It was a chilly November night, dark, clear and with no wind. The cemetery was quiet except for the sound of an occasional car passing by. Ron carried the cooler with our six pack inside. It was the first anniversary of Pat's passing, and we went to have a beer with him. Betty had a camera. "I can't believe you really brought that!" I said, surprised. Betty explained that the week before she had seen a program about a man who had gotten white fog on his pictures when he took them in a cemetery. Because of the "Mollie Pictures" Betty said, "Here Linda, you're the one who takes pictures of ghosts."

"You ARE crazy!" I said as I reached hesitantly for the camera. I began shooting, taking the first three pictures about fifteen seconds apart. It didn't take long to use up the twelve exposure film. At least we weren't wasting too much money. She could have bought a twenty-four or thirty-six exposure. Betty insisted that I take the film in the next day for finishing, so I promised her that I would go to a one-hour film processing place near my home. She also made me promise I would call her as soon as I picked the pictures up whether something showed up on them or not. Sometimes I got so irritated with her persistence.

I dropped the film off at the photo store and returned one hour later to retrieve the pictures. As I walked to my van, I asked myself whether I should look at the pictures now or wait until I got home. What would I do if something appeared on the pictures? What the hell, I had nothing to be afraid of, but I locked the van doors anyway. When I got to the second picture in the small stack, my breath left by body. BLUE FOG! Thoughts of the "Mollie Pictures" came flooding back. Just what was going on?

"Blue Fog" taken November 10, 1994

There had to be an explanation. Taking pictures in a cemetery at night was crazy enough, but this was crazier. Okay, I had to breathe. Bad film, Betty's camera, this "one-hour developing crap"...I'd figure it out.

I returned to the photo store and began questioning the person who had handled my film. I was no stranger to him. He was a close friend of my daughter's and answered my questions patiently but with a raised eyebrow. He carefully examind the negative and the "blue fog" could also be seen there. The machine that did the developing had not caused the problem. A discussion followed on the type of camera and film used. I explained to him that it was a 35mm point-and-shoot camera and the film was four hundred speed.

"Has the camera ever produced this effect before?" he asked.

"No," I answered. Betty would have told me. Her specific reason for bringing the camera had been in the hopes of capturing fog in the cemetery like the guy on television. I just can't believe we did!"

"Well, this could simply be ground fog. What were the conditions last night?" he asked.

"Clear and calm. No fog what-so-ever."

"Cigarette smoke?"

"No one was smoking," I answered. He could not suggest anything else. He didn't have a clue what the "blue fog" could be. First thing when I got home, I called Betty. "You're not going to believe this!" We discussed how we needed a plan. I was just sure that it must have been a fluke.

He smiled. He had their attention!

CHAPTER 8
THE "FACE"

There is a fifth dimension beyond that which is known to man. It is a dimension as vast as space and as timeless as infinity. It is the middle ground between light and shadow, between science and superstition, and it lies between the pit of man's fears and the summit of his knowledge. This is the dimension of imagination. It is an area we call the Twilight Zone.

Rod Serling, *Twilight Zone,* 1955-1963

We had to try and determine whether there had been something wrong with Betty's camera (I still thought that possible), something wrong with the picture taker (I found that one hard to believe), or if weather conditions might have played a part in the strange "blue fog." And one other thing not to be overlooked...was it possible that November 10, being the anniversary of Pat's death explain the strange picture? Now that this day had passed, maybe we would never get another one.

When we went back to visit the cemetery, there would be three cameras this time being operated by three different people; Betty, Lynn and I. What I didn't realize at the time, was how slowly and subtly I was being drawn into an incredible journey that I had not asked for. It was for definite that Betty had been "sucked in," which was okay for her, but it certainly was inappropriate for my skeptical nature. I did have to admit though, that if something showed up on our return trip, Betty wouldn't be the only one feeling the suction. So, there we were the very next evening, cameras loaded. The sun finally gave way to the moon (we all felt that ghost-hunting should be done in the dark!) and we headed for the cemetery. The weather conditions were identical to the night before. With three cameras flashing, the scene reminded of me of paparazzi minus the celebrities. I snapped one picture right after another and within minutes, informed the others I was out of film.

"Why do you shoot so quick? I'm only half done with my film," Betty said.

I explained to her that if something were going to appear, it would not matter how long we stood there. Everyone eventually used up their film, agreed to use their own developers and report back the next day. Lynn was not going to be able to supply a report, because she dropped her camera and broke it before we left the cemetery. So much for planning! Betty's results would be "nothing unusual," as were mine. The "Blue Fog" had been a fluke so, our cemetery picture taking days were over! Until...

...One week later, while I was cleaning up the house, I came across the photo envelope and decided to check it out one more time before throwing it away. There in the back of the envelope was a smaller one, a "Helpful Hints" sleeve, containing a ruined photo. The remarks to explain what had gone wrong reported that: "the shutter speed was not fast enough to stop action." For whatever reason, I saved it and gave it to Betty that night at our weekly gathering. "What's the whiteness in the picture?" she asked. I told her I had absolutely no idea, but it sure didn't look like a ghost. When Betty got the picture home she casually tossed it onto her coffee table, and gave it no more thought.

The next day, Rachel was visiting Betty and glanced at the picture sitting on the table in front of her. "Oh my God, I see a face!" she exclaimed. Betty carefully listened to her describe what she had seen and in a cautioning tone reminded her not to get to carried away. She continued to explain that she had just been going through some of Pat's old photos, and came across one of just half his face and that's why the "ruined" picture had caught her eye. Betty agreed that maybe half a face was possible, but she was still mostly absorbed with the odd whiteness. It seemed to

Taken November 11, 1994

her to be originating from Pat's grave site.

Two days later when we got together, Betty asked to see the negative. When she held it up to the light, she exploded, "Oh my God, there is a WHOLE face here!"

"What? Give me that!" I said skeptically. Betty was right. There on the negative was an entire face! All my nerve endings were screaming a response. Just who the hell was in my picture? No one was near me when I ended my roll of film! How was I going to rationalize this one to the skeptic sharing my body! The developer had indeed printed only half of our picture because it was actually a negative and a half. The rest of the picture had to be developed, but I hesitated going back to the same developer for fear that something would happen to the negative. The believer inside me cautioned that if the negative were truly that of an unexplained phenomena, it had to be handled carefully. What if it went into the developing machine and never came out? The picture would be lost. Did anyone have a picture so dramatic? I didn't think so, but I finally settled down and convinced myself that my friend would take special care of the only proof I had.

My friend greeted me as I entered the photo shop with a smirk on his face, "What now Linda, got some more ghost pictures? Ha!"

"Just tell me something," I began as I handed him the negative. He laid it on his counter light for examination. "Why didn't you print my *whole* picture?" His expression was priceless, as I watched the color of his face turn "white as a ghost." He assured me I would have my reprint in ten minutes. I returned exactly ten minutes later and as he saw me come in he went to grab my picture. IT WAS GONE! He went over to another counter, and...IT WAS NOT THERE! My heart was pounding. I could feel someone or something winding me tighter and tighter. My breath was coming in short bursts and the room was starting to spin. SOMEONE HAD ABSCONDED WITH MY NEGATIVE! I was in a panic! I just knew I should have used a

The “Face” taken November 11, 1994

more high profile developer! What I had feared had become a reality. Was I psychic? Hell no! This was pure human incompetence! My panic became contagious, in his haste to calm me, my friend suddenly looked down in the garbage can, and there lay the negative with the reprint ripped in half. Someone had mistaken them for rejects and had thrown them away! With an enormous sigh of relief, he said, "I'll have them for you in five minutes." This time I didn't leave the store, and I watched every move he made. When he showed me the results, we were both in awe. Just who was this a picture of? It didn't look exactly like Pat. I called Betty immediately from a pay phone and told her to get over to my house right away.

Betty made it over in record time and with barely one foot in the door, I rushed at her dangling the picture. "I could just snap you in two, you little turd. Just what have you gotten me into?" I blurted. I had been sucked into the "middle ground," the one between light and shadow and between science and superstition. I had entered the "Zone" and Betty had paid for my ticket!

"My God, Linda, he was standing right in front of you! If ghosts had to breathe, he would have fogged up your camera lens!"

"That's probably why the picture looks so hazy," I fired back sarcastically. "Listen, if I had SEEN that face through my camera, I would have been in the car and heading for the border. If this IS really a ghost, can you believe we got flesh-colored skin and pink lips? This is really weird!" But the BIG question had become, WHO or WHAT had been standing in front of me?

"What did the photo guy tell you?" Betty asked.

"It really threw him, big time. He said he had never seen a negative and a half before and after looking carefully at the negative he was pretty sure it's not a double exposure. He thought it was odd that the left side of the face didn't line up with the right side. Look at the eyes and eyebrows. They're goofy!"

"The other thing that still bugs me is this white area.

What did he say that was?"

"He had no idea."

"You know Linda, besides the fact that it seems to start at Pat's grave, it looks like the face is forming from out of it. Look at the narrower end of it, where the white ends and the top of the head begins. I've heard that the soul leaves the body from that point. Do you suppose it re-enters the same way?"

"Are you saying that the whiteness is the energy needed to form itself?"

"Well, couldn't it be possible? That would explain why the photo place checked that the shutter speed was not fast enough to stop the motion. Energy moves fast!"

"I don't know. I have to admit that this picture really freaks me out, but there has to be a logical explanation for it." Switch on...my defense mechanism was activated. To both of us, the face somewhat resembled Tom, so I rationalized that maybe he had accidentally snapped a picture of himself and then, realized that made no sense because, my film had rewound in the cemetery. He hadn't been there. Then I turned the picture upside down.

"My God, it's not a ghost, it's an alien! And if you cover up what looks like an alien, you can see yet another profile of a face, a face that looks like Neanderthal Man!" I just knew this would set Betty's toes a tappin'. If she could mess with my head, I could mess with hers. Let her talk her way out of this one.

"Maybe some sort of door opened up," she began calmly without missing a beat. My attempt to rile her had failed. "And we had a swarm of beings trying to communicate with us all at once. I read somewhere that when it becomes possible to communicate with this world, many will try at one time. Lets stay open-minded."

"To what? Space men and dead cave dwellers? You read too much."

"Linda, the image looks a little drawn out. Do you think you could pull the distorted image together in your computer? Maybe, then, we might be able to find out who it is." I told her I would try, but I was sure that my computer wasn't sophisticated enough. We had, after all, tried it once before.

"I'm going to bring the picture to some other photo shops and see what I can find out, and my friend in Eau Claire, who is a professional photographer, I'll show it to him. (I would find out later that he couldn't explain it either.) We both agreed we had to keep asking questions and in the mean time my older son, Andy, the computer "guru" and I did the best we could to alter and clean up the image, but didn't gain very much from our efforts. By the time I got back to Betty, she had already come up with out next plan.

CHAPTER 9
THE "WHITE BODY"

Science has long realized that all life energies are electric in nature. In my view, human personality is also made up of such energy particles. They are put together differently with each individual, resulting in the great variety of human character, but they are all working the same way...as carriers of personality, thoughts, feelings, and expressions.

Electrical impulses are capable of being recorded and measured. The "presence" of ghosts has already been proven with equipment designed along Geiger-counter lines. But I had always wanted to go one step further and prove these beings pictorially. Psychic photography is the answer. Ever since ordinary wet plates were invented and cameras used, there has also been an interest in photographing the Unseen.

Hans Holzer, *Hans Holzer's Haunted Houses*,
Crown Publishers, 1971

"We take my video camera, too!" Betty exclaimed. "Comprehensive, that's the word. Lynn, Betty, Rachel and I went to this shoot. The plan was simple, let Betty's video camera run while I took pictures. Putting the plan into action, though, proved to be another story. When we arrived at the cemetery, well after dark, we discovered that the path we always drove in on had been barricaded at all three entries by a big saw horse type barricade. The reason it posed such a problem was that Betty's video camera had neither a stand nor a light. "Come on Lynn, help me move this barricade," I stated matter of factly.

"You know, what's with you and moving things in cemeteries?" Lynn asked. I could tell she was tense, but this time she wasn't talking me out of it.

"This isn't a felony like the last time," I started my

defense. "All we need to do is move it to the side, pull your truck into position, take some pictures, and move the barricade back. No harm done. Besides I've been a member of this church for years, they've never barricaded the path before. There must be a new guy on staff. And look, people have done worse than this in the name of science. Now come on!" She folded and helped me move the barricade. Betty pulled the truck into position. We left the headlights on and started the camera rolling.

It always seems the case here in Minnesota, that when there's something important to do and the important thing to do is outside, it's winter. Take for example cars. They absolutely never breakdown in the summertime! And now we are picture-taking in a cemetery and no surprise, it was cold. Thank God, the wind wasn't blowing, and thank God, I had gotten all my anger out for Pat leaving us like he did...I might have stomped all over his site again. Of course, I had to remember this was really Betty's doing. "Here, Linda, take pictures." Then I had to laugh; I was there, wasn't I?

We let the camera run for about twenty minutes. Just as before, we experienced nothing out of the ordinary, saw nothing, felt nothing. We all "God blessed Pat" packed up our stuff, replaced the barricade and left. The four of us went back to my house, anxious to view what the video camera might have recorded, but then we ran into another barricade, as it were...trying to get Betty's video camera hooked up to play back through my TV. Wires and electrical connections have never been my thing. Like the time I tried to rewire a lamp by myself, I got all the little wire ends connected to something (it didn't seem too terribly important to what) and went to plug it into the wall. The first two tries caused the circuit breaker to pop; on the third time, I had smoke and flames coming out of the outlet. After that, plugging in anything, whether direct current was involved or not, would send a momentary chill up my spine with a brief reminder of how I nearly burned the house down or worse, electrocuted myself.

No direct current this time, but all the cords had to plug into somewhere and the problem was, there were too many holes to pick from. By the time we got the whole technical thing figured out, Betty and I were alone; the other two had given up. The only "visions" to appear on the film were the four of us and what visions we were. There we stood, in living color, bundled up and constantly shifting our weight from one leg to another in a fruitless attempt to stay warm. "Cecil B. DeMille move over! The Graham sisters have filmed the world's next great epic!" Betty and I laughed so hard we couldn't catch our breath.

Because of the holiday, Betty couldn't take the roll of film to be developed until Friday morning. It was important that *she* take it in this time to see what would happen with a different developer. Her son Jimmy went with her to pick up the pictures. The sales representative at the store pulled out the pictures and tried to explain to Betty what had gone wrong during picture taking. "It looks like your camera strap got in the way in this picture," she said and continued, "And the rest, well, someone must have had gloves on and they got in the way of the lens."

"Mom, you've got another ghost!" Jimmy whispered in her ear. Betty told the lady "Thank you" to be polite, but the whole time the woman was talking, Betty was remembering something from the video...*Linda had taken her gloves off.*

"Look Mom, it's a body!" Jimmy exclaimed. "It looks like he's either getting up or digging a hole!" All twelve pictures showed a strange whiteness in the lower right corner. Some showed more than others. The fifth picture taken on the roll showed a smoky appearance along with the solid white in the corner and then picture number six showed what appeared to be the complete top half of a body and the only picture that didn't have white in the corner. Betty went wild with excitement. "Wait till Linda sees this," she said to her son. "What possible expla-

The night before Thanksgiving, November 22, 1994

The "White Body," November 22, 1994

nation will she come up with this time?" she said with just a hint of smugness.

When Betty showed me the picture, I was amazed. As we examined it closer...

"Look, Betty, at the coiled appearance in the arm and the haziness to the right of the image. It appears to be in motion!" I exclaimed. "And another thing, in the center of the body, you can almost see what looks like a spine." I had seen nothing through the lens of the camera, so, just what was it that the camera had seen and the rest of us didn't? Somewhere deep inside me I figured I could blame Betty for all this. She and her whims. My logic and common sense were on the hot seat. Until recently, I had gotten along great with the scientific community... "everything in its place." But, Betty's ability to look at things with less complication and more emotion was going to "tick me off." The dead were dead, and I didn't want my world changed.

CHAPTER 10
THE "CONCURRENT PICTURES"

Photographs of ghosts or haunted areas are much rarer because of the great element of chance in obtaining any results at all. Whereas psychic photography in the experimental sense is subject to schedules and human plans, the taking of ghost pictures is not. We still don't know all of the conditions that make these extraordinary photographs possible and, until we do, obtaining them will be a hit-and-miss affair at best. But the fact that genuine photographs of what are commonly called ghosts have been taken by a number of people is food for serious thought.

Hans Holzer, *Psychic Photography: Threshold of a New Science?*, Drake Publishers, 1976

Betty always got irritated with me when I would quickly take one picture after another. My reasoning was that the apparitions would appear on one picture but not the next or the one before. It would seem that whatever was happening, was happening quickly. Here one minute and gone the next. What obviously made the investigation so difficult, was our inability to see what the camera was seeing. So I came up with another idea. This time, I would bring two friends with me to the cemetery, each bringing their own cameras, and try to get them to snap their pictures at exactly the same time. If something were there, would both cameras capture it?

Only a couple of weeks had passed since our video outing. Betty couldn't join us, so there were just three of us that night, two friends and myself. A little snow had fallen, but the air was again clear; it was not windy and the barricades were gone. We easily entered and drove directly to Pat's site. The two friends stood a couple of feet apart and readied their cameras. One was shooting one thousand speed film, the other four hundred. I stood near the grave and began the count-down. Three, two, one... they were supposed to have pressed their buttons when I said "one." You know, it's really funny how two people can hear something at the same time and not respond at the same time. The mind is really peculiar. I guess a few seconds apart shouldn't make a difference. Close enough as they say for "government work." We continued to shoot until we ran out of film. Some simultaneously and some separately. The following day, I went for developing. This time I would use someone different.

How many times would we continue to be surprised? The first photos taken from each one of the cameras showed a foggy appearance! The first photo shows lesser fog while the second seemed to show a shape taking form. Damn, this was frustrating. If only *we* could see what the camera saw. But one thing was for sure, the white fog was visible in two pictures, taken seconds apart, by two different people and two different cameras. Out of fifty-six pictures taken that evening, ten of them, in no special order and by no one camera, had the smoky appearance on them. At this point, I really wasn't sure what I thought, but I have to admit it was exciting. It would sure seem that we had taken "ghost pictures," but I wasn't ready to believe that it was Pat. I had no idea who it was. But the biggest question was WHY? What was the reason? What was the message?

Both pictures taken seconds apart, January,1995

CHAPTER 11
THE "BOARD"

Ouija...a board and pointer used for divination and by some as a means to contact spirits or entities. The name comes from the French and German words for "yes," oui and ja (ja is mispronounced with a hard "j"). Critics of the Ouija, who include authorities in most denominations of Christianity, say it is dangerous and a tool of the Devil. Advocates say that it, like other forms of divination, is a legitimate means to discover insight, wisdom, and self-truths and to communicate with discarnate beings.

Rosemary Guiley, *Harper's Encyclopedia of Mystical and Paranormal Experience,* 1991

What I ultimately wanted, was someone to point blank look at me and say..."Yes, this is what it is, and this is what it means." The order that I demand in my life would accept nothing less. The bottom line was that this had to be happening for a reason, so I tried to be open-minded to any and all possibilities. This was no longer just an adventure, it had become a mission.

For the past few months, I had started to consider the idea of using a Ouija Board. My strong Catholic background "reared wildly" deep inside me. This certainly was not a decision to be made lightly, for I had seen many movies and had heard many stories about the evils of the board. Could devils use unsuspecting participants to gain access into our world by creating a doorway to pass through? The board and its pointer were only made of wood. How could those inanimate objects be either good or bad? What I believed could make them evil had to come from the mind of the user. My motives, of course, were not evil, but still, I said nothing to Betty. I had shocked her when I agreed to the psychic encounter, so now the both-feet-on-the-ground-sister was contemplating a Ouija Board? I had to guard my position and integrity in the sibling hierarchy.

Betty and I had taken the winter off from shooting more pictures, but every time we got together we always commented on them. Finally, one day in April, 1995, Betty suggested we try the Ouija Board. She had heard that it was considered simply to be a very crude form of communication with the spirit world. If we couldn't get our answers from this world maybe it was time to give the other side a try. She hesitated to approach me. "Linda, let's try the Ouija Board." Betty said with caution.

"I've thought about that myself."

"I can't believe it!" There it was, Betty was shocked. "Are you really sure?"

"Why not? We're doing an investigation. We might as well explore everything, but I have to admit, a part of me doesn't think this is right nor do I think we can really get any answer from the beyond." There, my position was safe. "We need to keep things in perspective." Betty agreed and we split the cost of the board. We spoke to no one about our upcoming experiment.

Lynn, Betty and I met at Lynn's house, and said nothing to anyone about our plans for the evening. Our husbands and children would figure that we had gone over the edge, so secrecy had to be maintained. I wish I could say...*It was the darkest night I could ever remember except for the lightning that tore through the very soul of the darkness; that the thunder's deep rumble shook the windows trying to loosen the glass from its puttied resting place; that the wind howled its threats to rip the walls apart, reach in and tear our throats out...*but I can't. No added drama from the atmosphere. It was just plain dark. That would have to do. We lit a candle and started with a prayer that the experience be from and of God. I was taking no chances.

I'll be damned; the pointer moved with Lynn and me barely

touching its surface with our finger tips. If it had been anyone other than myself, I would never have believed it. Fear grabbed us for a moment as we both lifted our fingers from its surface. With wide eyes we stared in disbelief at each other. Then Betty wanted to give it a try, convinced that Lynn and I were messing with her head. To her surprise, she in combination with either of us got some movement, but not quite as dramatic as the movement experienced by Lynn and me. We weren't sure what that meant, but continued our experiment. For forty-five minutes we tried to contact Pat, but could not get a positive response. Experts will say that the pointer moves as a result of energy generated in the minds of the users. I was, therefore, surprised that if that were the case, why wouldn't the darn thing move accordingly? We WERE thinking of Pat.

When we finally gave up on talking to Pat, we asked to talk with anyone and the goofy, little three cornered piece of plastic jumped to life with one "yes" response after another. It would seem we were in contact with a spirit who called himself the Baron. He said he had followed Lynn and me from Georgia and said he was the image in the "Mollie Pictures." He further revealed that the pictures we took in the cemetery were to pique our curiosity and get us to use the board in an attempt to find some answers. The Baron wanted to speak to us.

"Our mission, should we decide to accept it" was that I should write a book with Betty's help. It was to be a Georgia love story and the Baron would be the main character...a lost soul in search through time for the love he left behind. He would help. He would be the "ghost" writer.

With our first experience seeming to be so positive, we consulted the "board" on two more occasions. The Baron, suddenly appeared unable to spell and finally admitted to being able to lie. What a joke, only I wasn't laughing. This was getting us nowhere.

It made no difference whether the pointer moved due to mind-created energy or spirits on the other side, its information could no more be verified or trusted than the psychic's claims. I do believe, though, that some good can come from all things, no matter how bad. The board had rekindled an old flame in me...to write.

"Been there, done that!" Our Ouija Board days were over!

CHAPTER 12
RAT TAPE

Two are better than one because they have a good return for their labor. For if either of them falls, the one will lift up his companion. But woe to the one who falls when there is not another to lift him up.

God, *The Holy Bible*, Ecclesiastes 4:9-10

By the end of May 1995, Betty and I were not getting along very well. With my marriage over, my increased social activities, and in her mind, my poor choice of a *new* relationship left her feeling pushed to the side. She was convinced she meant nothing to me. This was the first time the two of us had had such a long term dispute. Sisters have quarrels, but this one was a doozy!

I made several attempts to make things right between us, but at times she, too, could be very bullheaded and refused to soften her position. She was just sure that she could make the dispute last longer than the one Pat and I had years before. Three times I tried. Finally, at the beginning of August, I decided to have a talk with Pat. If he were truly in a place where he could help and God would let him, I sure needed it. This rift had to be closed. I never realized how quickly it would happen. It began with another dream and...

By Betty

...Betty's dream and subsequent events will be told by her...
Pound...pound...pound. "What is that pounding and where is Pat?" I asked as I entered through his front door looking for him.

"Out back," his housekeeper rudely replied. Why Pat needed a housekeeper is way beyond me. Quickly, I went out the back door. Pound...pound...pound. I looked up at the telephone pole, and there I found Pat pounding away at the top. I had no

idea what he was doing but seeing him squatting up there and swinging a hammer seemed ridiculous. "What are you doing?" I asked.

"Betty," he said, "go to the hardware store and get me some rat tape."

Ignoring his silly request, I nagged him again about his hired help. "Why don't you get rid of your housekeeper? I don't like her," I said flatly.

"Aghh," he groaned, bringing his arm in a downward motion that told me to just let it go. "Just get me some rat tape!"

"Rat tape?" I asked. "What for?"

"Just go and get me some."

"All right, I'll be right back."

As I backed down his driveway my dream ended.

The next morning I pondered the dream. "What in the world is rat tape?" I asked myself. I had never heard there was such a thing so I decided to keep this dream to myself.

Two days later, while I was alone at work in the dental office getting caught up on paperwork, I got up from my desk to go the back room. As I rounded the corner of my desk, the smell of a man's cologne hit me. I stopped for a moment, dismissed it and continued to go into the back room. A few minutes later I returned to my desk and it hit me again. *Cologne*. "By God, where is this coming from?" I said aloud to myself. I got on my hands and knees smelled the floor and the carpet. Nothing. The walls smelled like walls and the carpet like carpet. The odor was simply in the air. Then as quickly as I noticed it, it was gone.

The next day, my daughter Laura and I were sitting on the couch channel surfing, when I stopped abruptly on a show about a giant rat destroying a house. My dream came rushing back, so I decided to share it with her. She agreed it was strange and laughed at the thought of Pat sitting on a pole and swinging a hammer. Later that same day, while watching some rented videos, one of my cats, who was napping peacefully on my lap, lifted her head and vigorously sniffed the air. Then I smelled it. A man's cologne hung thick in the air. That was the strongest I had ever smelled it! "Jim, did you use that smelly deodorant today?" I asked already knowing what the answer would be. The onset of the fragrance had been too sudden.

"No, Mom," he answered. "But I smell cologne too."

"Laura, did you spray yourself with perfume?" I continued to investigate.

"No, I didn't," she hollered back. That's it, had to be my husband, Craig.

"I smell it too," he said returning from the kitchen. "I just didn't want to say anything." He sure didn't want any part of unexplained phenomena. One in the family was enough. The aroma lingered about a minute and then was completely gone. The cat lowered its head and returned to the nap she had been taking. We looked at each other puzzled. Well, now I wasn't alone. If I were nuts, it was a sure thing that my whole family had caught it... "nutphobitis!" Even the cat had it. Craig thought I should call the doctor for ointment!

The following weekend, our neighbors invited us to Duluth for the annual *Blues Festival*. Our neighbor's mother, Millie, had a beautiful home right on Lake Superior and said that we could park our motor home in her driveway. From the first time we met, I had always felt a special connection to Millie, so I was really looking forward to the visit. After the concert, we all sat in Millie's living room listening to her stories. Millie had so many great stories to share about her life and never losing her southern accent made them even more entertaining. One of her stories hit me like a freight train. Not a train lolly gagging through a busy city making drivers wait much too long at the crossing gates, but one that is moving at "Mach 2" and one can just imagine the engineer with his hair on fire.

Millie's story began with the death of a friend. Millie had offered to go in and help pack up and clean her friend's home. This friend in life had been a bit eccentric and had collected food the same way some collect baseball cards. "Imagine all the varmints, honey," she exclaimed to me, "We sure could of used a lot of rat tape in that house."

"Excuse me?" I asked stunned. "Did you just say *rat tape?*" *The train whistle screeched its approach.*

"Oh, yes dear. That place was a mess. Creatures runnin' to and fro," she said.

"You mean there is such a thing?" *Another long blast from the whistle.*

"Sure, it's sticky tape you lay on the floor and when the little buggers run 'cross it they stick like glue. Great stuff," she laughed. *WHAM! Well, scrape ME off the tracks!* How could I dream of a product I have never heard of, and a week later I'm discussing it with my neighbor's mother? Pat was playing with me again! His fingerprints were all over this...his wild sense of humor.

The next night, when we got home from our trip, I had another dream. This time, I was having an uneasy dream of the tension surrounding my quarrel with Linda when Pat popped up out of nowhere and stood in front of me. He was so close to me and his attitude was so peaceful and happy.

"I absolve you," he said with his arm pushing toward me like a faith healer. He just stood there looking at me. I thought: this isn't very funny, Pat. I had expected him to make me laugh, and then "poof" he was gone. I woke up with my eyes wide open. It was one o'clock in the morning. "What the hell was that about?" I questioned to myself. "And why didn't our mouths move? Had we communicated by thought? Weird." The next morning, the first thing I did was get a dictionary. Just what did "absolve" mean? *To let it go, it never happened, to set free*. Why didn't he use the word forgive? That word is more familiar to me. And why absolve me, when it's Linda who should be absolved?

That same morning, I had a hair appointment which just happened to be across the street from Linda's house. Up until now, I'd had no intention of speaking to her, but wouldn't it be a shocker to go knock on her door? Should I or shouldn't I? Making the first move is always hard, especially when you think you were right. But, Pat's message had been clear: "enough certainly was enough." With my appointment finished, I went to her house. When she answered the door I said, "I absolve you!" I extended my arm as Pat's had been. I then started to laugh because of the look on Linda's face! She was not yet amused (she of course believed she wasn't wrong either) but invited me in. "Rat Tape" had been a remarkable dream, and its impact on Linda and me would last a life time. Pat's two sisters were friends again.

CHAPTER 13
DELIVERANCE

Many people believe that they have a spirit guide or guardian angel. This celestial being accompanies and assists a person in various ways. For most people this help appears as a hunch or a subtle feeling that comes over them. Other individuals claim to be in conscious contact with their guides at all times. Volumes have been written delineating case histories of people whose lives have benefited from this kind of intervention.

Hazel M. Denning, Ph.D., *True Hauntings*,
Llewellyn Publishing, 1996

Betty's "Rat Tape" dream...The foundation of my well-constructed fortress named "Skepticism" was slowly crumbling and surprisingly, I wasn't scrambling to make repairs. The dream and its conclusion were real, solid facts and there was no way I could discount their validity, nor did I want too. With peace restored, we could once again continue our investigation.

Our next "shoot" was on the second anniversary of Pat's passing. This Minnesota November evening was a lot colder than the year before and the "aura," as Betty says, "was all wrong." As always, we began our observance with a prayer and snapped some pictures. When the film was developed, the only unusual thing to appear was in the upper left corner of one photo. The oddity was white and oval shaped. In the world of the paranormal, this would be defined as a "spherical spirit" and it is supposed to be rare to get this type of phenomena on film. (Someone else told us it could be a portal...gateway to the "other side!") This was to be only the first of many Betty and I would see in our pictures. We both had to admit, though, that these circular images were not nearly as impressive as our other pictures, but we did at least get something.

Taken in November, 1995

The only way to explain why the "aura" was all wrong might be to consider just how messed up my aura probably was and how messed up Betty's was by close association. By November, my immediate concerns were not on getting strange pictures in the cemetery, but on self preservation. I will go briefly into the story, not in an attempt to tell a "stalking" story (although, God knows it could be a complete book in itself), but to tell of two events that happened as a result that are important to this effort.

Betty had been right about my new relationship with a long-time friend of fourteen years. When he had re-entered my life I was excited, but with Betty's warnings, I had remained cautious at the same time. By November, this relationship could best be defined as one person (him) trying to have total power and control over the other (me). Freedom, independence and being myself had become the major thrusts in my life. I had been through and learned too much in forty years to throw it away now. If this guy needed to dominate, he would have to find someone else. Saying he got angry when I told him this would be an understatement. The guy got vicious and wild. For two months he stalked and harassed me. Filthy cards and letters came in the mail; tires of family and friends were slashed, a wrench was thrown through my patio door, threats were made to burn down my house; there were also constant drive-bys, and hundreds of annoying calls. For the first time, I feared for my life and the lives of everyone close to me. I made sure that all of these incidents were documented with the authorities and they assured me that they would eventually catch him.

The new year, 1996, was looking anything but hopeful until one very clear and cold January night. After many calls and drive-bys by the stalker, the police set up a stake out in the hopes of nailing him once and for all. Feeling safe, I took two sleeping pills at one thirty in the morning and went to bed. Just before falling asleep, I asked Pat to protect me and help bring this nightmare to an end. Three hours later, I awoke from a sound sleep for no apparent reason, except for a nagging feeling that something was about to happen. I got up, went downstairs checked all the doors and windows and peered outside to see if anything looked wrong. I settled myself by remembering that Coon Rapids' finest were on the job. (What I didn't know at the time, was that with the shift change, all the stake out personnel had been pulled off duty an hour before.) I thought I had nothing to worry about, so I returned to bed twenty minutes later. At five minutes to five, I sat straight up in bed to a crashing sound coming from downstairs. Without even taking time to put on my robe, I ran down the stairs and looked through the window in my front door. There standing in my driveway was my stalker and in my living room was shattered glass and a hammer. I yelled to my oldest son, Andy, who had his room downstairs, that this guy was in the driveway. Because of his training and experience as a licensed protection officer and law enforcement student, he was out the door within seconds, trying to stop the intruder. In his right hand he had a gun and a cigarette in his left. All he wore was a pair of boxer shorts. The quiet night was awakened with "Ahhhhhhhh!" bellowing from his mouth as he chased the car for half a block. I stayed inside and got 911 on the phone. Andy returned frustrated that he hadn't been able to catch him, because his bare feet kept slipping on the hard packed snow and ice. What amazed me was that he still had both the gun and cigarette clutched in his hands. In just ten minutes, four squads had pulled the stalker over. In the front seat of his car they found two long knives. He was finally arrested.

A short time later, an officer came to my door to make the report on my damaged window. I could have kissed him. He told me that when he radioed to the station that this guy had been caught, "A cheer went up. You would have thought the Vikings had made a touch down." I wasn't the only one that wanted this person locked up. As he finished his report he added, "It's nice to win one every once in awhile." What were the odds that I would wake up three hours after taking two sleeping pills? If I hadn't been awake, I never would have gotten down the stairs in time to see him in my driveway. Being too keyed up to sleep, my sons and I decided to go out for a celebration breakfast. As I stared out the window of the restaurant thinking of the night's events, I saw a large blue cement truck (identical to the one Pat used to drive) go down the highway. For just a moment my breath stopped. In all the years I have lived in Coon Rapids (nearly twenty) I can't recall ever seeing his company's trucks this far north. Was it just a coincidence to see one that particular morning? I smiled and quietly thanked Pat for his help and blessed him.

Then, two days later, while Tom and I were watching television, I smelled it...a man's cologne. I knew I wasn't nuts, because Tom smelled it too. It lasted just a minute or so and then was gone. Again, I smiled. The skeptic in me was just about gone. Pat seemed to be just around the corner. Could God have assigned him to be my guardian angel?

CHAPTER 14
"NEVER SAY NEVER!"

I can't believe I'm doing this again!

Linda Graham, *Pictures, Dreams and Visits,*
Gramus Publishing, 1997

Betty approached me in May suggesting that we consult another psychic. She had heard of a whole family of them that lived right here in Minneapolis. Red flags went up and so did my blood pressure. I could hear...*never again, never again* ...repeat itself over and over in my head. Betty, of course, admitted that the first experience had been a total disaster, but she reminded me that it wasn't fair to judge the entire psychic community on that one experience. She was right, but it didn't matter. I flatly refused.

A couple of weeks later, I was showing our pictures to a friend. She was really impressed with them and suggested that I show them to an acquaintance of hers who dealt with this type of phenomena. I was shocked to learn that the person she was speaking of was the same person Betty had mentioned weeks earlier. My friend assured me that this psychic was reputable and that it would be well worth my time talking to her.

I let Betty know that I may have been a little hasty in not agreeing to see this local psychic. I told her I would call and make an appointment. After several attempts, I finally reached her by phone only to find out, that she no longer did readings. The major part of her current activities was to rid homes, institutions, etc. of unwanted spirits but she did agree to at least look at our pictures. The meeting took place mid-May at a small coffee shop in south Minneapolis.

"Definitely spirits here," the psychic began. "Fantastic pictures, I can't believe how many you have." She went on to explain how the bad spirits will appear on film as gray or black in color and nice spirits appear white. The ones appearing gray or black have probably committed suicide and or are afraid they will be sent to hell. They choose to be earthbound. Spirits move very quickly and can be the reason they appear on one picture and not the next. They are not photographed unless they want to be.

Often times, the spirit will be seen with a head and no body, or a body with no head, (like the "Mollie Pictures.") It struck me that with all the "dehauntings" she did, that the photographer who went with her had yet to get a picture. For this reason she asked us if we would be interested in sharing our pictures and story in her upcoming book. This Betty and I had not been prepared for. We were just beginning to think that we could do our own book. We declined her offer. Her guess as to the reason why we were getting these pictures was to let everyone know that the dead were still with us. There is life after death and they are not far away. Her final instructions...TAKE MORE PICTURES!

My friend did not realize that her acquaintance had stopped doing readings and because she felt that it was important for Betty and me to have a reading, she recommended another. The fee for this reading was half the dollar amount of my reading two years earlier and this lady was going to let me tape the session. It would seem she had nothing to hide, so I thought maybe this time we might have a chance to know the truth, or maybe part of it anyway. What eventually did happen was only slightly different from my first experience.

Betty and I drove to her home and sat with her at her dining room table. I expected to see all kinds of "psychic/spirit" things hanging on the walls and objects representing the beyond sitting on tables, but there was little. This psychic and her environment seemed normal.

She told us that she had consulted her spirit guide before we arrived and began the reading with assessments of both Betty and me. I am, according to the spirits, supposed to develop my personal gifts and Betty is to take more time for herself and wrap herself in purple light every morning. These directions were to bring us greater peace in our lives. So here was the generic kick-off. None of these things can be proved or disproved. Red flags had already gone up in my mind and were waving wildly, but we needed to get to the pictures.

The only tool she used during our session was a string of crystals. As she identified each picture, she did so by holding the crystals above each picture, pausing for a moment, and then announcing what appeared in the picture. Of course, the response was always the same, "strong spirit activity." Having no knowledge of Pat's passing, I asked her who the spirits were and what did they want. She said the spirits were a group of massacred Indians. They were not buried there, but it seemed to her that they had passed through what later became a cemetery, on their way to their deaths. Indians, now *that* had never occurred to me. I wonder why!

When I asked if she could tell us anything about Pat, she had no idea who we were talking about. Betty and I shared a glance and with no words we knew what each other was thinking..specifics were going to be a problem. For all practical purposes the reading was over. We did stay a while longer out of curiosity and the human need to get our money's worth. After filling in a lot of blanks for her, she told us Pat was stuck and couldn't move on. His soul travel was interrupted. He had been my late night visitor, the one who caused Betty's kitchen to shake and was currently hanging around in Betty's basement...reason for the cologne smell.

"With the cat litter box?" Betty asked stunned and then followed with the answer to her own question, "I don't think so."

"What message does he have for us?" I asked.

"I'm not quite sure. I would have to go to Betty's house

and ask him," the psychic answered. There would be, of course, a fee because she wouldn't go just to talk to him, she would need to send him on his way.

"Can't the spirit guide tell you what the message is?" Betty prodded.

"No, It must not be for your highest good right now to know, so the spirit guide isn't saying. This doesn't happen often. I just don't know." The psychic quickly changed the subject and drew our attention to the photos showing our circular images. As she dangled her crystals over the top of them, she reported that this was definite "alien" activity. Hearing me let out a "Humph," she said "This activity is real and right now there are two space ships parked over Minneapolis. Ours is a violent planet. They are here to help. They tried to protect you at the power plant, but had not been successful. That's the reason the fog dissipated so quickly."

From various sources of information, Betty theorized that it might be possible that electrical energy aided the spirits in taking form and being visible to people or cameras. It is reported by some that an electric magnetic field will be disrupted where there is spirit activity. This sub power station is located just behind the cemetery. Imagine our surprise when the smoky appearance showed up on our pictures. The four were taken in approximately three minutes and show the quick dissipation of the unusual phenomena. (I photographed two other sub plants located in Coon Rapids and nothing unusual appeared.)

"And, Betty, the spirit guide has told me that it is time for you to know; you have been alien-abducted. These abductions began at the age of four. They planted a metal tracking device in your head," she said as she turned her head and parted her hair in the back to reveal the approximate location.

"They have since taken the metal plate out because they have finished with you and now is the time for you to clear yourself

The following four pictures were taken within three minutes and in the order they appear.

of these events so you can develop your third eye," she said as she pointed to the space between her eyes. Totally dumbfounded, my head made a sharp snap in Betty's direction to see her reaction and immediately saw the shock and disbelief. Her "aura" had gone from calm purple to fiery red! She attempted to maintain herself with some "oh's" and "huh, huh's" but I could tell she was frantic inside. If she had said I had been alien-abducted, it would have been easier for me to just "blow it off" right away, but I knew Betty would have a problem dismissing the ridiculous suggestion. That did it! This psychic had picked on the wrong sister. You know, you can only kick yourself so many times. I had always known, deep down, that a psychic would say spirit activity but the alien stuff had been an unexpected twist. I will not speculate anymore than to say that life on other planets I've always thought possible. The very size of the universe would suggest we are probably not alone. What was so frustrating was the fact that this psychic, like the other, spoke only in generalities and anything that sounded like a statement of fact, i.e. pictures of spirits, pictures of aliens, could not be disputed. The bottom line has always been, "Say what you want, believe what you will." My gut feeling at this point was that Betty and I already had our answer, but to be thorough we needed to give science a try. Trying to stay objective was going to be hard. I just knew what the "people of science" were going to say.

Once again, I found myself calling the University of Minnesota. This time I needed to reach someone in the photography department. The phone was answered by a professor, who told me that the mechanics of film developing and the camera itself could better be explained by a professional in the field. Her expertise was in picture composition, color, light, etc. She directed me to a photo lab in downtown Minneapolis. Anyone who is anyone goes there for their photographic needs. They were specialists.

CHAPTER 15
LINT, LENS, LEAKAGE and LIGHTS

A STRANGE WORLD

Something strange is going on. We live in a world whose realities are defined by science, which tells us how things work. And yet there are some things which don't seem to work that way at all. Our science tells us that these things are impossible and don't exist, yet they stubbornly refuse to go away. There are relatively few of them and they are often elusive and hard to control, but they are there for anyone to see. They exist.

Lyall Watson, *Beyond Supernature*, 1988

Betty and I arrived fifteen minutes early for our appointment. Just who could figure the traffic that day. No one. Downtown Minneapolis was usually a driver's worst nightmare, especially for a driver like me who only negotiated the area once every couple of years. The gentleman we were to meet with was named Mark and he was tied up in an interview, so we were asked to wait. This was indeed the finest photo place I had ever been in. On entering the building, to our right was a large office area; directly in front of us was a long service desk staffed with four people; to our left, behind a glass wall was a room full of many machines both large and small. Each machine was being operated by a person who had "capability" written all over their face. We were so impressed! What a far cry from the small photo shops we were used to.

With the time we had, Betty and I looked over our negatives making sure that everything was in order for our meeting. This was obviously a very professional place. We needed to have our ducks in a row. A woman came over and asked if we were the ones that had phoned the day before about some unexplained pictures. It would seem that word of our visit had spread fast through the lab and within minutes, a large group of employees had gathered around us as we began a brief explanation while they looked at our pictures. Even a couple of curious customers joined the group. The excitement came to an abrupt halt, when the boss, Mark, walked over to our area. This is not to say that he was harsh, it was just very clear that this was the person in charge. He was personable and direct. I guessed him to be middle-aged and he said he had been with the lab a number of years. We needed someone with experience. Mark also admitted he was a skeptic, but would do his best to give us honest answers. I was confident we had come to the right place.

Our time with him went quickly. He looked at all of our pictures and thoroughly examined each negative. We discussed with him faulty equipment, light leaks, double exposure, faulty development or printing, chemical spots, reflections, refractions, lens flares, aperture, weather conditions and, finally the picture takers themselves. He offered several thoughts on how to produce artificially or duplicate what appeared on the pictures, but Betty and I assured him that all we did was point and shoot. Quite honestly, we admitted lacking the knowledge to be able to fake such appearances. Our photographic expertise consisted of modestly priced cameras that did everything automatically: focusing, light etc. Anything more complicated than lining up the shot and pushing down the button was more than either of us cared to deal with.

We told Mark that six different cameras and five different photo finishers had been used. The odds that all six cameras were defective and five photo finishers inept were staggering. We have all used our cameras many other times and have never gotten such strange apparitions...they appear only when we shoot in that cemetery. (Three of us were in England two years ago, reportedly one of the most haunted places on earth, with the same cameras used in the cemetery and out of approximately six hundred pictures taken by the three of us, not one oddity showed up on any of them! We even took a "ghost tour," at night, in Edinburgh, Scotland and got nothing. Although, I would have settled for a picture of Sean Connery!)

As an afterthought Mark suggested the possibility of a dirty lens or maybe fuzz balls from a mitten. It had been cold on many of our outings. He made this claim based mostly on the "White Body" picture. We explained to him how careful we had been when taking the pictures. It was, after all, an experiment and even though we can't boast of sterile conditions, we did make sure that camera straps, fingers, and clean lens were given proper attention. Our video tape, taken the night we got the "White Body," showed me taking off my gloves. Mark then added it would be highly unlikely that fuzz or dust would take on such a distinctive shape.

By the end of our meeting, even Mark's skeptical foundation was also cracking a bit. In his many photographic years he had come to see many strange pictures. Some similar to ours, especially the ones with a smoky appearance. Some he could explain and some he could not, but one thing was for sure, he said he would always remember ours.

Betty and I sought continued evaluation from two other photographers. One of them was an ex-military man who had done photo reconnaissance for the Navy. His comments were similar to Mark's, but he helped us better understand the causes of peculiar effects that will sometimes appear on pictures. He discussed; "lens flare," our circular images, but also told us it would be rare to have this occur at night, since the sun has much to do with it; "radiant energy," as possibly the reason for our "power plant pictures," but said that to capture that on film would be a phenomenon in itself; then came the "Face." At first glance he thought it looked like a double exposure, but couldn't be sure.

The whiteness on the picture bothered him more because he had no idea what could have caused it...no more of an idea than what caused the "white body." Whiteness in pictures indicates exposure, but how the whiteness came to appear in our pictures he had no idea.

The third opinion we received was from a photographic expert from North Minneapolis. Our biggest concern had become whether or not to add the "Face" picture to our book. We were afraid at that point to have our credibility questioned because of a photo that, when first glanced at looked like a double exposure. The first two photographers agreed it looked like one but couldn't really say for sure, so we found one more expert before we made our final decision. The expert we found was not just highly regarded in the photographic world, but was one half of a team the does psychic photography. Betty and I explained the circumstances that surrounded how the photo was taken (how the film had rewound in the cemetery etc.) She examined the negative thoroughly and concluded that it was not a double exposure. She marveled at all the wonderful pictures and encouraged us to pursue our goal. "This type of phenomena is showing up more and more frequently today and I'm not quite sure why," she reported, "But it certainly seems to me that your brother is having a lot of fun with you." Betty and I agreed that our two year journey had indeed been fun and we finally had our answer. It had become very clear to us that...*Explanations are relative and opinions are subjective*. It was a fact that the "Face" picture had taken us to the next level of our investigation, so double exposure or not, it was an important element of our story.

CHAPTER 16
"TAKE MORE PICTURES"

The important thing to remember about psychic photography is that the bulk of it occurred unexpectedly and often embarrassingly to amateur photographers not the least bit interested in parapsychology or any form of occultism. The extras on the negatives were not placed there by these people to confuse themselves.

Hans Holzer, *Psychic Photography: Threshold of a New Science?*, Drake Publishers, 1976

The following pictures were all taken in the Summer of 1996...

This picture shows what appears to be a "moving" sphere just off to the left of our brother's grave site. A smaller one can also be seen to the right of the larger one. One other strange occurrence that particular night was the strong scent of a man's cologne filtering through the air, which we never experienced in the cemetery before, nor have we since. These random occurrences only support the uniqueness of each event.

These photos were taken one right after another, seconds apart with one camera. The first picture shows a small brown sphere near the right edge of the picture. In the very next picture, taken seconds later, the movement of the sphere can be seen clearly as it came to rest near me. We were excited to have finally achieved a long awaited goal...to get two pictures in a row showing the movement of an apparition. In addition to this, the photographers who evaluated these photos were especially puzzled by the brown color. The pictures before and after these two were totally clear of all phenomena.

This picture shows a strange white appearance (just above the grave stone next to Pat's site) and the fuzziness on the left of the shape would seem to indicate it was in motion. I returned the next day, to rule out reflection. No explanation could be found.

CHAPTER 17
THE "GERMAN SHEPHERD"

Jesus tells us that the angels of heaven have their eyes on every person. They know the spiritual condition of everybody on the face of the earth. Not only does God love you, but the angels love you too. They are anxious for you to repent and turn to Christ for salvation before it is too late. They know the terrible dangers of hell that lie ahead. They want you to turn toward heaven, but they know that this is a decision that you and you alone will have to make.

Billy Graham, *The Collected Works of Billy Graham*,
Inspirational Press, 1993

We had taken our photographs to specialists in photography who gave us their theories of lint, lens and lights, and to the psychic community which found them to represent spirits and alien activity. We were now ready to give the religious sector a look. Logically, of course, the church we chose for this religious opinion was the one that shared ground with the cemetery itself. The denomination is Catholic, and directly behind the church and to the north of its administration building sits this quiet, peaceful, pretty little cemetery. It was only fair to give the pastor of this church a chance to respond to our two years of research; although, we both suspected the Church would tell us it was the work of the devil. For this reason I hesitated to schedule this meeting, for Betty and I were convinced that our events were not evil in nature, and I didn't want the phenomena to stop by the sprinkling of Holy Water. Taking the risk at this point really didn't matter because we already had plenty of great pictures!

This priest we were about to see can be a bit intimidating as I well know from working with him for over fifteen years, so it was important again to have all our ducks in a row. When it really counts though, his gifts of compassion, understanding and sensitivity are second to no one. (This is the same man who stopped me from collapsing on a hospital floor and blessed Pat repeatedly into the next life.) He doesn't dismiss the grief experienced by the loss of a loved one, but has a very special way of helping anyone in mourning to celebrate death. He gives gentle reminders that their absence is temporary, that we will someday be joined with them, and that although they may be out of sight, their existence continues in a much more magnificent place. We should all celebrate their joy. Father is a stout man whose hand shake is nothing less than bone crushing. He has left many a young buck wondering where his strength comes from.

"The Lord!" he laughs. "You ought to give Him a try!" His gray hair reflects over seventy years of wisdom and experience and he can truly say "been there, done that." But, had he ever seen ghost pictures? Betty and I hoped not. We love to be able to catch the good Father off guard and figured this might be a challenge no one else had given him. So, the time had come to meet with the good Father, who is one hundred percent German and the leader of a parish with a population greater than that of most small towns across our country, nearly nineteen thousand parishioners...Father Reiser, the "German Shepherd."

The appointment was made for Thanksgiving night. Holidays afford a little quiet time at the Rectory with parishioners busy with family gatherings and not making calls to the Church. So, with just a couple of minor changes in our dinner schedule, Betty and I met with him at eight o'clock, assuming little interruption to our meeting. Walking into Father Reiser's office immediately causes sensory overload. It was very easy to see how much this man was admired by the many people he administered to. It was a very large office with a big wooden desk with a large executive style chair behind it. I smiled when I remembered a cartoon I saw some years ago...*it pictured an executive who had fallen over backwards in his chair, so only his feet could be seen sticking up from behind the desk. The caption read, "Who told anyone to grease my wheels?"*...The walls were covered with cherished items; family pictures, plaques of all sizes and shapes proclaiming various rules for living and thoughts for meditation, a huge wooden rosary and a collection of baseball caps with funny sayings and of course, his Minnesota Twins baseball cap. The tables were loaded with knick-knacks and statues. On his desk was his Snoopy phone, a gum ball machine and piles of paper. In fact the papers were not just on his desk, they were under his desk, behind his desk, on the side of his desk and across the room from his desk! It reminded me of my sainted mother who, being German, also saved everything.

"So Father," I began, "we have some pictures we'd like to share with you."

Picture by picture we told our story. I wasn't sure which word was going trigger his bolt to the door with Holy Water in hand, but to my surprise, his reaction was quite the opposite. He thought the pictures were remarkable and combined with our dreams and other experiences, he felt something very special was going on. There was absolutely no reason to suspect that "evil" was behind it. He told us he had seen the works of both good and evil. Many times he had been called to rid homes of activity which threatened harm. He often heard stories of people nearly hit when ashtrays, books and other objects, for no reason, launched themselves across a room. Some reported a terror felt from the sound of unexplained footsteps, draperies flapping (not from the wind) and dark images seen floating about a room. In each case, Father would go to the home, do a special blessing and all of the fearful activity would stop. Some of these people were long time friends of his and parishioners that he knew to be average, down-to-earth and intelligent...Betty quickly interrupted with, "Oh, like Linda and me?" she smiled slyly. Father wasn't about to get caught off guard, so he quickly agreed with a roguish grin.

"Your story, though, is not a story of malevolence," Father continued. He reminded us of the many Biblical accounts of spirits and the people that saw them, and told us of his firm belief that angels can take human form and walk with us on earth. I was surprised to hear him say that spirits and angels are sent by God all of the time to help us. That was certainly not the impression the Church had given me all these years. He explained that everyone needs a higher level of awareness to the events and people around them, because that kindly stranger just might be an angel sent by God to help us achieve our ultimate goal...Heaven."

"You believe this to be contact from the other side then?" I asked.

"I certainly can't state that for a fact, but the evidence would seem to point in that direction," he continued. "For the believer, death is just another chapter in that great experience of an individual's life. Our stay on planet earth can be short, or very long, but all lengths are very short in comparison to our stay in eternity, which will never end. For Almighty God, death is a natural consequence of being born. We need to be born into this world to be alive, and we need to die to be born into eternity. Life doesn't end, it changes. None of us can be sure just how interactive the next life can be with ours, but just picking up a newspaper or turning on the television should help explain why the time has never been more right for direct intervention from the "other side;" these occurrences are on the rise, both locally and world-wide. The appearances of Mary are most prominently heard of, but Father also knew a six year old boy who regularly saw the Holy Family and the messages were always the same, "pray and prepare, for we will all be held accountable for our own thoughts and actions."

As we neared the ending of our hour with Father, he returned thoughtfully to the pictures and told Betty and me that we had been given a special opportunity for spiritual growth. We would need to continue to look deep inside ourselves for continued answers. I then told him how the psychics had interpreted our pictures. His head didn't move, only his eyes with elevated eyebrows looked at us over the top of his glasses. He said, "Some are good, and some are not. Be careful and remember they have built themselves a billion dollar business. Beyond anything more specific," he said looking at Betty, "if you should 'pass on' any time soon, you be sure to let us know the details!" The roguish grin was back.

"You bet I will," she replied. "And by the way, we have reserved three more holes (plots) in the cemetery, right next to Pat's: one for Linda, one for Craig and one for me. So, if we all go before you, be sure to come out with your camera and take pictures. You just never know with all of us there, what will show up!"

"I'll bet you never knew you had a party section out there, did you?" I laughed.

As Father walked us to the door, we promised to show him any future pictures. The meeting with the German Shepherd had gone well. Betty and I made one final stop before going home. It was at the cemetery to..."take more pictures!" We were both pleasantly surprised when the next day after picking up our developed film that one of the pictures showed a smoky appearance. Not since the "Concurrent Pictures" (almost two years ago) had this anomaly appeared. Were we getting a thumbs up from the other side?

Taken on Thanksgiving November, 1996

EPILOGUE
JANUARY, 1997

Legend has it that when the gods made the human race, they fell to arguing where to put the answers to life so the humans would have to search for them.

One god said, "Let's put the answers on top of a mountain. They will never look for them there."

"No," said the others. "They'll find them right away."

Another god said, "Let's put them in the center of the earth. They will never look for them there."

"No," said the others. "They'll find them right away."

Then another spoke, "Let's put them in the bottom of the sea. They will never look for them there."

"No," said the others. "They'll find them right away."

Silence fell...

After a while another god spoke, "We can put the answers to life within them. They will never look for them there."

And so they did that.

Marie-Louise VonFranz, *The Way of the Dream*,
Shambhala Publishing, 1992

Why did we get these pictures?
Who or what are in the pictures?
Are they pictures of ghosts?
Why only this cemetery at this site?
Is there a message?
What is the message?
Did six cameras malfunction?
Did five different developers make mistakes?
Is it lint, light leakage or lens flare...?
Is it radiant energy?
Did we have a *Close Encounter of the Third Kind*?
Are there spaceships parked over Minneapolis?

Did we take pictures of aliens?
Can psychics really communicate with the other side?
Can anyone communicate with the other side?
Where did the cologne smells come from?
What or who pushed on my bed three times?
Why did Betty's house rumble three days in a row?
Why did it rumble at exactly 5:24 each day?
How did the restaurant ticket appear in Betty's car three days later?
Is the number three significant?
How could Betty dream of something she had no knowledge of?
How did the department store bag roll across the living room floor?
How could a bag maneuver two corners and end up by Betty's bed?
Was the malfunction of the car computer a message?
If it was a malfunction, why hasn't it happened since?
How did I wake up so soon after taking two sleeping pills and catch my stalker?
Did all the upheaval surrounding Pat's death play a part?
Did he leave us with too many unspoken words and unsettled matters?
Do spirits and angels walk among us?
What is the meaning of life???

Betty and I know what we think. Now, what do you think?

The End. Or is it?

One final thought...

The following was brought to our attention by our Aunt Alma.

I thank you for the love you each have shown,
but now it's time I traveled on alone.

So grieve a while for me, if grieve you must,
then let your grief be comforted by trust.

It's only a while that we must part,
so bless the memories within your heart.

I won't be far away, for life goes on.
So if you need me, call and I will hear.

-Author Unknown

WE WANT TO HEAR FROM YOU!

Because so many people have had their own experiences to share with Betty and I, we have decided to write another book based on some of your unexplained *Pictures, Dreams and Visits.* Write your experiences and/or send any pictures you might have to the address below. We will choose the accounts we feel are most suitable. If we select yours, we will notify you by mail, so please don't forget to include your address.

Everyone's identity will be protected at all times.

Gramus Publishing
P.O. Box 48187
Coon Rapids, Minnesota 55448-0187
USA

* * * * * * * * * * * * * *

Need more copies of Pictures, Dreams and Visits: A True Story. For a personal autographed copy, mail the form below.

Please Print

Name____________________________________

Address__________________________________

City/State/Zip______________________________

Autographed to______________________________

Please send me________(quantity) books@ $13.95 each $__________

Postage and handling (Add $2.50 per book) $__________

Sales tax (where applicable) $__________

Total amount enclosed $__________

Send check or money order (no cash or CODs) to:
Gramus Publishing, P.O. Box 48187, Coon Rapids, MN 55448-0187
Please allow 4 - 6 weeks for delivery.
Prices subject to change without notice. Valid in the U.S. only